Praise for

STRATEGY FIRST

"Brad Chase is an early Strategy First mentor of mine. He taught me the fundamentals of Strategy = E × mc², which have helped guide me as I've founded, run, and advised many technology businesses. I'll bet he can help you, too."

—RICH BARTON, CEO, Zillow Group

"Effective, real-world storytelling enables *Strategy First* to drive home the importance of establishing strategic priorities before taking action—a highly practical reference for any serious business leader."

—JIM ATTWOOD, Managing Director, The Carlyle Group

"A successful strategist isn't afraid to make big bets—because behind every move is forethought, evaluation, and planning. I've known Brad for decades, and seen firsthand how his inventive model has driven success for some of Microsoft's most important initiatives. *Strategy First* is full of incredible advice on understanding opportunities and competition from a pioneer in his field."

—MELISSA WAGGENER ZORKIN, Global CEO and Founder, WE Communications

"*Strategy First* captures thousands of hours of experience in a couple hundred pages, offering instantly useful frameworks for focusing on what matters most: strategy."

—**ELENA DONIO,** CEO Axiom

"Brad is a long-time colleague. This book helps you think about your business in the most important way—strategically. It's full of compelling real-life examples that you'll enjoy reading and learn from."

—**BRAD SILVERBERG,** Co-founder Fuel Capital, Co-founder Ignition Partners, and former Senior Vice President Microsoft

"Using a clever twist of Einstein's $E = mc^2$ formula, Brad Chase delivers essential elements for business leaders seeking the most relevant, yet elusive success factor of all . . . strategy. Filled with the captivating stories of some of the most successful strategic moves in business history, you'll find practical reminders and inspiration on each page for squaring up on your customer focus to win. No matter the size of your business, this read serves as a healthy reminder that winning big does not happen by chance; it requires calculated actions to begin with."

—**KURT FRAESE,** President, Fraese and Associates, and former CEO, GeoEngineers, Inc.

"*Strategy First* is a fun, important read that serves as a guidebook for any business leader."

—**JOHN OPPENHEIMER,** Founder and CEO, Columbia Hospitality, Inc.

"It's probably universally accepted that failing to plan is really planning to fail, yet planning to win is still a neglected exercise. Brad Chase's *Strategy First* offers the first truly practical approach to strategy development—a method that is simple, effective, and sustainable."

—**BILL HATHAWAY**, Founder and CEO, MoreSteam

"Brad Chase's *Strategy First* is an ingenious take on a complex topic. His strategy formula is easy to remember and to apply, and the many examples he cites will make a long-lasting imprint on the reader. If you are, or want to be, in business, treat yourself to this book. You'll carry its message with you long after you've read it."

—**JIM HORGDAL**, President, Brink's Global Service USA

"Brad's *Strategy First* approach is 'ready to use,' practical strategy advice from a guy who has led, guided, and observed successful strategies across a wide spectrum of companies and products. You can put it to work right away."

—**PETE HIGGINS**, Partner, Second Avenue Partners, and former Group Vice President, Microsoft

"Whether your business is just a concept or a start-up or an emerging enterprise or even an incumbent—read this book! Because inside you will find insight, reflection, and wisdom to get you focused on what really matters—your strategy."

—**BRENDON RILEY**, Chief Executive, Telstra InfraCo

"With *Strategy First*, Brad Chase provides a practical formula, principles and perspectives to enable informed decision making. Coupled with stories and examples, Brad shares a portfolio of tools that will be valuable for leaders across multiple industries."

—**CLYDE WALKER**, Board Chair, First Choice Health

"As a member of the Brooks Board, Brad brought this powerful framework for building competitive brand strategy to us at an important time in our journey. The clarity of thinking he brings to solving the customer puzzle is refreshing."

—**JIM WEBER**, CEO, Brooks Running Company

"Brad's new book is a great read, but particularly so for anyone who wants gain a creative perspective on strategic thinking. With his riff on Einstein's theory of relatively, Brad smartly reminds us what matters most in any strategy: the value your customer finds in your product. After outlining the rest of the model, he brings the concepts to life with many relevant and familiar examples across a wide range of industries. Along the way, the reader will get a chance to gain an insider's view of some of the biggest strategic bets Microsoft ever made."

—**CHARLIE BALL**, Executive Vice President, Holland America Group

"Brad Chase's sharp-witted storytelling underscores effective strategizing for a new era."

—**DEANNA OPPENHEIMER**, Founder, CameoWorks and BoardReady

"Having worked with Brad at Microsoft, it's great to see that he has decided to share his *Strategy First* model with everyone. It proved to be a game-changer for Microsoft. It will be for you, too. Don't miss out!"

—**TONY AUDINO,** Founder and CEO, Conenza, and Founder, Microsoft Alumni Network

STRATEGY

1

FIRST

Ernest Chase

BRAD CHASE

STRATEGY

FIRST

HOW BUSINESSES WIN BIG

GREENLEAF
BOOK GROUP PRESS

Published by Greenleaf Book Group Press
Austin, Texas
www.gbgpress.com

Distributed by Greenleaf Book Group

For ordering information or special discounts for bulk purchases, please contact Greenleaf Book Group at PO Box 91869, Austin, TX 78709, 512.891.6100.

Design and composition by Greenleaf Book Group
Cover design by Greenleaf Book Group
Cover images used under license from ©Shutterstock.com/Art Stocker
Interior illustrations by Alicia Thornber
Interior images used under license from ©Shutterstock.com/Wstockstudio, ©Shutterstock.com/OoddySmile Studio, ©Shutterstock.com/Christian Delbert, and ©Shutterstock.com/Lucie Lang
Interior images may not be reproduced without written permission from the author

Publisher's Cataloging-in-Publication data is available.

Print ISBN: 978-1-62634-712-0

eBook ISBN: 978-1-62634-713-7

Part of the Tree Neutral® program, which offsets the number of trees consumed in the production and printing of this book by taking proactive steps, such as planting trees in direct proportion to the number of trees used: www.treeneutral.com

TreeNeutral

Printed in the United States of America on acid-free paper

20 21 22 23 24 25   10 9 8 7 6 5 4 3 2 1

First Edition

To my family

CONTENTS

Foreword

When I joined Microsoft in the early 1990s, the company was abuzz with energy and anticipation centered around a project with the code name "Chicago." It would become better known as Windows 95, and it would transform the still-young software industry.

In those days, it was impossible not to be aware of a marketing leader whose team was driving the launch of Windows 95, a product that in many ways ushered personal computers into the consumer mainstream. It was a great product designed with an intense focus on the customer, and the marketing strategy felt very much like a movie blockbuster. Microsoft licensed the Rolling Stones' song "Start Me Up" for its first ever product-centered TV commercials, and late-night talk show host Jay Leno emceed the launch event. We lit up the Empire State Building with the Windows logo colors. And there was a well-orchestrated, substantive set of activities that included customer training, co-marketing with partners, and the largest beta test that had ever been conducted for a piece of software. Windows 95 went on to break all sorts of sales records, and Brad and his marketing team won countless awards for their efforts.

I later joined Brad's team after he was asked to help turn around MSN, Microsoft's internet service and search engine. The service was struggling to gain customers and was losing money—not surprising given the MSN groups' low morale, a failure to focus on culture, and the lack of a strategy. Change was needed, and that's what Brad led: a turnaround story he tells in *Strategy First*.

During his review of the teams and projects at MSN, he recognized that there was an opportunity to weave together the many services within the MSN group into a cohesive, compelling set of internet services for small business. Brad bet on me to figure out the details and asked me to come back to him with a proposal. From that was born bCentral, a set of web services for small businesses and startups.

From these and other experiences, Brad advances the theory that execution, market potential, and customer value are essential to landing the right business strategy. His battle-tested approach is attracting audiences in business schools and in boardrooms. Deservedly so. When I became CEO of Microsoft, I raised a lot of similar questions. What is our mission, and what is the culture and strategy to achieve it?

As I wrote in my own book, *Hit Refresh*, we must recognize that when we are an inch apart on strategy at the leadership level, our product teams end up miles apart in execution. Getting strategy right—centering innovation on customer needs—must preoccupy every leader from start to finish.

All of us are in business to meet the unmet and unarticulated needs of customers. That's what innovation is about. Successful strategies have empathy for customers front and center, and they are aware of competitor efforts to get there first. Product design requires deep empathy, a customer obsession. And our colleagues, our partners, must feel that they are empowered to build customer-first strategies.

Brad shares keen insights and helpful tools, from defining key elements of a strategy to activating and executing those elements. It is also a book for those, like me, with a passion for the history and economics underlying industrial development.

In *Strategy First*, Brad outlines some of the tips that have helped him in his highly impactful career and reinforces the centrality of building winning strategies.

—Satya Nadella

INTRODUCTION

Two of the Most Successful Business Bets in History

In the spring of 1987, as a student at the Kellogg School of Management at Northwestern University just outside of Chicago, I traveled to Seattle three times. The first time was for a day of interviews at Microsoft. When Microsoft couldn't decide whether to hire me or not, they flew me out for a second day of interviews, which was quite unusual. I guess this second round of interviews went well because Jeff Raikes, who ran Applications Marketing at the time, made me a job offer that I accepted. The third trip was altogether different: along with other MBA hires—including Melinda French (the future Melinda Gates)—who would start their jobs in the fall, I flew to Seattle to attend the annual Applications Marketing offsite and sit in as the team discussed its strategy and plans.

This was 1987, before the internet, before wireless or mobile phones, and before computers had the speed and memory they have today. In fact, most computers ran MS-DOS (Microsoft Disk Operating System), a character-based operating system that controlled the essential operations of the computer, including disk management, keyboard control, video support, executing programs, and memory and file maintenance. Users would type commands to navigate the files and folders on their computer. To see a list of your files, you didn't open a folder by double-clicking the mouse to look at your file names but typed "dir" (for directory) at what was called the command prompt (c:\). Super intuitive!

The story behind Microsoft and MS-DOS is a dramatic one. Though it may be an urban legend, Thomas Watson, the president of IBM in 1943, supposedly said, "I think there is a world market for maybe five computers." Back then, a computer was a tube-powered calculator the size of a house. Of course, IBM figured out that Watson was wrong and built large mainframe computer systems like the System/360 (introduced in 1964) that helped turn IBM into a tech powerhouse. IBM dominated the industry through the 1970s with its mainframe prowess. Meanwhile, the personal computer market was beginning in the late 1970s with machines like the Apple II, Commodore PET 2001, and TRS-80 from RadioShack. Overall, the market was small, most users were hobbyists, and the operating system most computers used was called CP/M (Control Program for Microcomputers) made by Digital Research. At that time, most personal computer users also used, and therefore knew, computer languages. Microsoft, betting on the success of the personal computer, was the leading producer of personal computer languages like BASIC. That bet, the first of two successful bets I'll cover, was fundamental to the success of the company.

THE FIRST BET:
THE PERSONAL COMPUTER

Bill Gates and Paul Allen, the co-founders of Microsoft, famously penned the tagline, "A computer on every desk and in every home," which represented their belief that the personal computer market would grow dramatically and change the world. Internally, Bill and Paul used a slightly different tagline: "A computer on every desk and in every home running Microsoft software."

As the personal computer market continued to grow, IBM became interested. In the summer of 1980, IBM decided to develop the IBM PC. Because the personal computer market was growing so quickly, IBM set an ambitious goal to build and release the IBM PC within one year. Given the size and bureaucracy of IBM, that was a tall task, and IBM knew that the only way they had a chance to complete the product in such a short time frame was to use off-the-shelf components and license the software. Jack Sams, the director of software development for IBM, came to visit Microsoft to license its languages.

Everyone was betting IBM would quickly take a leadership position with the IBM PC when it shipped, and Microsoft was excited about the potential of an IBM deal. When it turned out that IBM needed an operating system too (something IBM thought incorrectly that Microsoft also had), Bill Gates, in the middle of the meeting, called Gary Kildall, the founder and CEO of Digital Research, and told him that he was sending some very important guys down to meet with him. Digital Research was the owner of CP/M. Shortly thereafter, Sams and the IBM team flew to Pacific Grove, California, to meet with Kildall.

You would assume that, like Microsoft, Kildall would have been super excited and would have moved heaven and earth to discuss the possibility of licensing CP/M to a business titan like IBM. Any deal with IBM would bring boatloads of cash to Digital Research. But Kildall wasn't interested. Kildall had already planned to fly with a friend on a private plane, and instead of changing his plans to accommodate IBM, Kildall's wife, Dorothy McEwen, who ran the company with Gary, attended the meeting.

Unlike Bill, who had signed the famously one-sided IBM nondisclosure agreement immediately, McEwen asked her lawyer to look at the IBM nondisclosure, and he balked at its restrictions. So IBM spent the whole day debating with lawyers and McEwen about whether they could even talk to each other without a signed nondisclosure agreement. Microsoft executive and future CEO Steve Ballmer put it in context: "Just imagine what it's like having IBM come to visit—it's like having the Queen drop by for tea, it's like having the Pope come by looking for advice, it's like a visit from God himself. And what did Gary and Dorothy do? They sent them away."[1]

So a frustrated IBM left Pacific Grove and went back to Microsoft to ask for help licensing an operating system that would work on the IBM PC. Paul Allen knew a developer named Tim Patterson who worked for Seattle Computer Products and had developed an operating system called QDOS that, with some additional development, would work for IBM. Microsoft seized the day, and in 1981 Microsoft bought QDOS from Seattle Computer Products for $50,000, plus some discount on upgrades of Microsoft languages, and renamed it MS-DOS (Microsoft Disk Operating System). Patterson went on to work for Microsoft, and together they did the necessary development work and then licensed MS-DOS to IBM. Microsoft agreed to provide MS-DOS for a flat fee to IBM and, to IBM's surprise, did not ask for a royalty but ingeniously made sure that their license with IBM was nonexclusive. Microsoft retained the exclusive right to license MS-DOS to other companies. The IBM PC launched to great success and fanfare in the summer of 1981, and because it was an open architecture, a slew of other PC manufacturers got into the business of building IBM "clones," which were essentially IBM-compatible PCs. Microsoft licensed MS-DOS to all of them, and MS-DOS quickly became the standard PC operating system and a cash cow for Microsoft.[2]

These watershed moments—Kildall blowing off a meeting with IBM to fly on a private jet, McEwen's unwillingness to accept IBM's nondisclosure agreement, and Bill Gates and Paul Allen buying QDOS and recognizing the strategic opportunity of owning the operating system for the personal computer—changed the entire course of the tech industry. The success of MS-DOS and the impact it had on the personal computer industry and Microsoft itself is hard to overestimate. Having a standard operating system that was essentially the same on most personal computers allowed software companies to build applications that would work the same on almost any computer. Similarly, companies would build hardware such as printers, keyboards, and hard disks that were compatible with MS-DOS. As more software and hardware was built to work with MS-DOS, customers had more

network effect

choices, prices came down, and MS-DOS computers became even more popular.

This "network effect" business where success breeds success helped lead to the immense popularity of the personal computer. Microsoft garnered a preponderance of its profits from MS-DOS because computer manufacturers needed it to run their computers and paid Microsoft a royalty for each personal computer sold. MS-DOS, bought for $50,000 and change, turned into a multibillion-dollar product and the financial juggernaut driving the success of Microsoft in the 1980s and the first half of the 1990s. Maybe the best business deal ever done.

Yet ironically, despite its enormous success, well before 1986 Microsoft was planning the death of MS-DOS.

THE SECOND BET: GUI

I first heard the details about the second big Microsoft bet at that offsite in 1987. Microsoft was working on Windows, a graphical user interface (GUI) operating system, that at first would use MS-DOS as its core but would introduce a whole new user experience, new improved features for managing files, and new computer hardware and memory. It would be the foundation for a whole new set of more powerful and easy-to-use GUI applications.

Pronounced "gooey," like the consistency of a great chocolate chip cookie, GUI is a visual way of interacting with a computer using devices such as a mouse to open and close windows and click on icons and menus. Sound familiar? Microsoft was also reluctantly working with IBM on another GUI operating system called OS/2. The problem was that IBM's goal for OS/2 was to displace Microsoft's leadership and profits from

operating systems. This time around, IBM wanted to control the operating system design and the licensing to other computer manufacturers.
So why did Microsoft work with IBM on it? Steve Ballmer explained:
"It was just part of, as we used to call it, the time riding the bear. You just
had to try to stay on the bear's back and the bear would twist and turn and
try to buck you and throw you, but darn, we were going to ride the bear
because . . . otherwise you would be under the bear, and in the computer
industry, IBM was the bear."[3] So in a way, Microsoft's bet on GUI had a
second option. Either Windows or OS/2, or perhaps both, would eventually replace MS-DOS altogether like how high-definition (HD) TV
replaced standard definition TV, and given the market power of IBM,
Microsoft was willing to work with them on a product that was not really
in Microsoft's best interest.

At the time of the offsite, when I was almost finished with business school, MS-DOS was the standard operating system for personal
computers, but when it came to applications, Microsoft Word was a
distant second to the most popular word processor: WordPerfect. And
Microsoft Multiplan was losing badly to Lotus 1-2-3, the dominant
spreadsheet software product on the market. But Microsoft had a plan.
Microsoft conceded that the company had little chance of overtaking
WordPerfect and Lotus 1-2-3 on MS-DOS. Both of those products
were deeply entrenched and popular with users of MS-DOS, and it was
just too difficult to come up with some new transcendent feature(s) that
would compel users to switch.

Instead, product managers like Jeff Sanderson and Phil Welt, and
leaders like the aforementioned Jeff Raikes, laid out a plan and placed
their bets on GUI: If the Microsoft applications were first and compelling when users made the material switch from MS-DOS to Windows

or OS/2, then users would also be prepared to switch away from Word-Perfect and Lotus 1-2-3 to Microsoft's more powerful, easy-to-use GUI applications for Windows or OS/2 like Microsoft Word and Microsoft's spreadsheet application, called Microsoft Excel. In poker terms, they were going all-in with a gigantic, risky, core strategic bet on GUI.

Microsoft had experience building GUI apps for the Apple Macintosh, which was a key advantage in developing Microsoft Word for Windows and Microsoft Excel for Windows and OS/2. The Apple Macintosh was an excellent computer but had a much smaller market share of computer sales in 1987. Apple made the strategic decision to not license its operating system software to other companies that built computers, like Microsoft did with MS-DOS and later Windows, and that decision was probably a mistake because Macs were only made by Apple and thus were more expensive, had fewer models, and had lower sales, and consequently there were fewer third-party software and hardware products available that worked on the Macintosh. But because the Mac always had a GUI design and was operated with a mouse and used icons, folders, windows, and so forth, it was consistent with the GUI strategy of the applications division, Microsoft had prioritized Mac applications years earlier. In fact, in 1987, the applications division of Microsoft ironically garnered more of its revenue from Mac applications than it did its MS-DOS applications. Microsoft Word, Microsoft Excel, and Microsoft Works (an all-in-one program that had a basic word processor, spreadsheet, and database combined in one product) were the top three Macintosh applications.

However, betting on users switching to Windows or OS/2 on the far more popular PC platform was a very, very risky bet. At the time of the offsite, the first version of Windows existed, but it was unpopular. Windows

2.0 was coming in December 1987, and it was an improvement, but it was still not a great product. OS/2 wasn't even released to the public at the time of the offsite, and its development was going poorly.

But while Windows kept improving, OS/2 development never got much better. Well after the offsite, with the passage of time, it became clear that Microsoft needed to make its GUI bet on Windows and Windows applications exclusively and not on OS/2 and OS/2 applications. OS/2 was not a good product, and it was a competitor to Windows. Though it was scary and risky, Bill Gates eventually decided Microsoft should no longer ride the bear. The success of Windows 3.0 in 1990 and IBM's unwillingness to support it led to the end of the Microsoft-IBM partnership in the early 1990s, which meant that OS/2 development fell exclusively to IBM. At this point, IBM OS/2 and Windows became official vigorous competitors. Microsoft was betting everything on Windows. "We are betting the company," Bill would often say. If Windows failed, the operating system business would be in big trouble, and the strategy of building Windows applications to overtake WordPerfect and Lotus 1-2-3 would also fail.

Or to put it more dramatically, if Windows failed, the dominoes would fall, and Microsoft was likely doomed.

Over the ensuing years, I helped, along with my colleagues throughout the company, as Microsoft executed on that simple GUI strategy. Windows 3.0, the first compelling version of Windows, was improved considerably with Windows 3.1 in 1991. Several years later, Microsoft released Windows 95 to massive acclaim and success, dramatically improving Windows, and its popularity ushered personal computers into the mainstream. The Microsoft applications team released multiple versions of Word for Windows and Excel for Windows before and after

Windows 3.0. Both products were well received in the marketplace and continued to be improved and updated through the 1990s and beyond. In the early 1990s, Microsoft Word and Microsoft Excel along with Microsoft PowerPoint, an application that helps create presentations, were combined on both the Mac and Windows operating systems to create Microsoft Office.

Meanwhile, despite being encouraged by Microsoft's Systems division to release its applications for Windows simultaneously with the introduction of Windows 3.0, neither WordPerfect nor Lotus was willing to make the same bet as Microsoft. WordPerfect 5.2 for Windows, the first well-developed version, wasn't released until November 1992. A planned new version of Lotus 1-2-3 developed to take full advantage of Windows was never completed at all. Lotus released a poor Windows adaptation of its existing spreadsheet in 1991—the only change was the use of a graphical interface. By the early 1990s, Microsoft was the leader in word processing and spreadsheets, and WordPerfect and Lotus were quickly on the decline.

And what about IBM and OS/2? IBM continued to develop the software through the mid-1990s, but it never achieved material sales or momentum, and in 1996, IBM closed the OS/2 development lab in Boca Raton and announced that over 1,300 people would lose their jobs. Under the weight of IBM's poor software design and development, IBM OS/2 failed.

Microsoft's original bet on the PC led to a bet on languages that led to a bet on operating systems and a multibillion-dollar MS-DOS business that fueled Microsoft's growth through the mid-1990s. A second bet on GUI ended up replacing the MS-DOS billion-dollar business with two multibillion-dollar businesses—Microsoft Windows and Microsoft

Office. Few bets in the history of business have been more consequential or successful.

STRATEGY FIRST

In the chapters to come, you'll see that placing big business bets can lead to big jackpots, if those bets are based on a winning strategy. Microsoft made two critical, bold bets, and both paid off because of the strategy behind them. The key lesson I learned from Bill Gates is that strategy is job number one—hence the title *Strategy First*.

Bill and Paul had a plan and knew precisely what they were trying to do. They knew their bets were risky, but they also knew the caliber and potential of their product. They knew the value of personal computers and how they'd one day earn their spot inside every business and home. But more importantly, they knew that the true value and business opportunity of the burgeoning PC industry came from software not hardware, so they focused Microsoft as a software company. And as a software company, they recognized the centrality and market potential of the operating system and mainstream applications. Finally, they knew that GUI was the interface of the future. Their strategy was layered with insight and ingenuity, and over time, backed by tens of thousands of development hours. In short, Microsoft planned its attack and then attacked its plan.

How can you do the same? How does one go about devising and executing a successful strategy? What do you need to do, learn, and understand in order to do so? How long until you can confidently make a bet and have it pay off?

I've scoured the library and the web and haven't found anything that provides simple, compelling, fun, and helpful insights into business strategy. I've seen nothing that offers an easy and memorable model to use that helps people think more strategically, nothing that explores different approaches to using that model or providing real life examples to hit the message home.

That's what I'm going to give you.

In this book, I share an easy-to-remember model that will help you think about strategy in a way that's not academic or intellectual but practical and memorable. I'll cover key elements to be considered when plotting and building your business strategy. I'll show you how the elements complement the model and which pieces are must-haves versus nice-to-haves. Things like seeking change or finding differentiated customer value; mining gaps by capitalizing on the spaces where competitors are underperforming or nonexistent; adapting to the tides and aligning your efforts with your external environment; expanding the universe and growing your business by understanding your customers and your market; and finally, climbing short walls and building tall walls or breaking into markets with low hurdles while constructing barriers to deter competition.

When we're done, I hope you not only gain a clear and comprehensive understanding of the centrality of strategy but also feel like you have the appropriate tools to move forward with executing a successful one. I hope you learn different ways to think about and approach your business endeavors, taking into account the common oversights that can either help or hinder your progress. I hope you find inspiration from the people and companies whose successes or failures have provided an invaluable road map for all of us to learn from. But mostly, I hope you have fun, are challenged and inspired to push new boundaries, and feel compelled to make big bets of your own that are backed by solid strategies.

PART I

KEY ELEMENTS OF A SUCCESSFUL STRATEGY

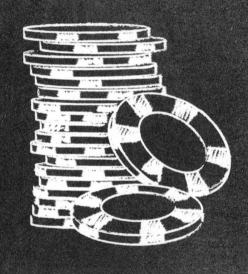

CHAPTER 1

The Strategy Imperative

When Marie Kondo's book, *The Life-Changing Magic of Tidying Up*, was first published in Japan in 2011, sales were pretty standard. Kondo was in her mid-twenties and worked at a staffing agency full time and as an organizational consultant on the side. But when Kondo's consultancy "side" job grew to have a months-long waiting list, she decided to make a big bet and quit her full-time job to focus on consulting. She wrote her book—loosely based on her college thesis, "How to Declutter Your Apartment—From a Sociological Perspective" in response to clients asking how they could learn about her method while they waited for their consultation.

Fast-forward to today and Kondo oversees a sprawling and multinational decluttering empire around the KonMari Method, her minimalism-inspired approach to tackling clutter category by category rather than room by room. As of 2019, she's authored four books (which have sold over 11 million copies and have been translated into 40 languages[1]), created an online database that connects people to certified organizational consultants, been named one of *Time* magazine's 100 Most Influential People in 2015, launched a lifestyle brand that includes a storage box collection that was sold out for months after its release in 2018, starred in her own Netflix series, and has a smartphone app under development.

How did this happen? How did she go from standard sales to a multi-millionaire magnate? What was her secret ingredient?

I have done countless speeches on strategy over the years at companies, conferences, and business schools. I always begin my speeches by asking questions, and there is one question I always ask the business leaders or MBA students in the audience: What is most important to the success of a business and a business leader?

Think about it. What would you say?

The problem with writing a book is that I can't hear your answer. There is no two-way dialogue with this medium (yet), but I can tell you some of the answers I often hear: vision, charisma, inspiration, communication, trust, values, empowerment, influence, process, sacrifice, empathy, compassion, power, emotional quotient, intelligence quotient, judgment, good people, and knowing your competition.

And obviously these attributes are super important, but I would claim that none of these are the right answer, not really. My contention is that creating a winning strategy is most important to the success of a business and a business leader. There is no successful company that doesn't have a successful strategy. Often the strategy is thoughtfully forged. Sometimes it comes from trial and error, and sometimes a successful strategy is dumb luck, but a winning strategy is the business success imperative. You can be charismatic, you can know your competition, you can have good judgment, you can hire the best people, and so on and so forth, but if your strategy fails, your business will fail. The MS-DOS, Microsoft Windows/Office story reinforces that.

THE "E" STRATEGY

My first couple of years working at Microsoft were spent on Microsoft Works for Macintosh (as I mentioned, Microsoft dominated Macintosh applications at the time), and then around 1990, I jumped over to be the first Microsoft Office group product manager before being asked to run the marketing for MS-DOS. At the time, MS-DOS was on millions of computers, but the only way to get a new version was to buy a new computer. When MS-DOS 5 was introduced, it was the first time a consumer could go to the store and buy an upgrade that, once installed, would take the old version of MS-DOS and replace it with a current version. I was tasked with overseeing the small marketing team that directed the MS-DOS 5 launch. We did a nice job, so much so that I was asked to run both the marketing and development for MS-DOS 6, the last big version of MS-DOS. When that was a success, I was offered the opportunity of a lifetime—to run point on marketing for Windows 95. It ended up being career transformative.

The launch of Windows 95 was comparable to that of the early versions of the iPhone. The hype surrounding it was crazy; it was the talk of the town, and to rein in the chaos around its release was a tall order. I knew, first and foremost, that it required a solid plan. I needed a sound marketing strategy. Since MS-DOS was no more, I reorganized the talented MS-DOS and Windows marketing teams into one Windows marketing team and then got to work figuring out how to pull the whole thing off.

Everybody wanted to know everything about Windows 95—users, partners, companies in the industry, the press, competitors—and there was an incredible pressure to make sure nothing got leaked. One night, I was working late after the kids were in bed, and the marketing strategy suddenly came to me: What if I turned everything on its head and opened the floodgates? Instead of trying to prevent everybody from knowing everything about Windows 95, what if we did the opposite? What if people got to know every last thing?

My theory was that if the marketing centered around everything the new software offered—a brand new easier graphical user experience with things like the start menu, the ability to run multiple programs simultaneously (preemptive multitasking), and plug and play so new add-ons to your PC (like a printer) would install and work seamlessly, to name just a few—then consumers, including the more engaged industry influentials, would be educated and privy to what was behind the curtain. In turn, they'd be engaged and excited and would bet on Windows 95. Plus, if the third-party community that wrote software programs, built hardware like computers, mice, and printers, and wrote books and training materials knew what to expect and were excited about it, then their products would come out earlier, taking advantage of the innovations in Windows 95 and giving people more reasons to move more quickly to Windows 95. If it all worked out the way I was thinking, perpetual motion would feed on itself and lead to success.

I called it the E strategy: Educate, Excite, and Engage. The goal? To make Windows 95 a consumer phenomenon. The execution? Imperative.

My marketing team was primarily organized by customer. One team focused on consumers, a second on business, a third on press, a fourth on partners like PC manufacturers and software developers, and a fifth on working with Microsoft's international teams outside the United States. Each team developed its "Educate, Excite, Engage" plan specific to its customers. For example, when it came to education, business users wanted to know about the costs and benefits of training employees to become proficient in the new user experience with the "start" button, so we developed those materials. Technical users and the industry press needed to know the detailed specifications and how more advanced features like networking would work, so we developed these materials, did countless press tours, and ran countless seminars. The general press needed reviewers' guides and product explanations, so we held a consumer press seminar to teach even very computer-novice press people how Windows 95 worked. We also did broad-based education, like distributing 10 million demo disks in computer magazines and running a 23-city Windows 95 preview tour to educate interested consumers about the product.

My boss, Brad Silverberg, the vice president and overall Windows 95 leader at the time, had the idea to run the largest beta test in software history, and my team added a broad preview where users could pay $20 to play with a test version of the product. In the end, over 400,000 users tried a test version of Windows 95 before the final version was released. The beta test helped the team find bugs and ensured that Windows 95 worked with older software and hardware, but from a marketing standpoint, the beta test and preview program got hundreds of thousands of people to try it out. It was free publicity, free insight into the perks of the product, and yet another one of the countless programs we ran as part of the "education" element of the strategy.

"Engage," in my terminology, was about getting the industry knowledgeable about and committed to shipping products for Windows 95. We did endless sales calls, training, and technical seminars so industry players could take advantage of the features of Windows 95 in their products and have them ready to go when we launched on August 24, 1995. We worked with PC manufacturers to ensure their PCs would be ready, as well as resellers so boxes of Windows 95 upgrades would be available the day of the launch. That timing was especially important because most stores ran midnight madness sales. Our intentional groundwork with partners led them to promote and spend money to market their product with Windows 95, like when GT Interactive did a video guide to Windows 95 featuring *Friends* stars Jennifer Aniston and Matthew Perry.

All the education and engagement activities created excitement for Windows 95, but we also turned up the hype machine as part of the "excitement" leg of the educate, excite, and engage stool. On the August 24th launch date, we lit up the Empire State Building in red, green, blue, and yellow—the colors of the Windows logo. We draped a 300-foot Windows 95 banner down the CN Tower in Toronto. We landed the new product on the cover of national news magazines, on TV and radio, and in the industry press. Basically, it was impossible not to know about Windows 95.

Of course, most of the attention Windows 95 received was not publicity we generated directly. For instance, Doonesbury ran a whole comic strip series making fun of Windows 95. When it hit ten days before launch, I told the team we had officially achieved our goal: Windows 95 was a consumer phenomenon. (I loved Doonesbury at the time and asked the PR agency to get me a signed copy of the strip, and Garry Trudeau was nice enough to oblige.)

START ME UP

To keep the excitement going after Windows 95 was launched, we wanted a big, bold advertising concept executed with an energetic but approachable campaign. We worked with a stellar ad agency that came up with the Start Me Up campaign, which hinged on the functionality of the brand-new start button as well as the Rolling Stones' 1981 hit of the same name. It was brilliant.

There was just one problem: The ad agency could only get the rights to "Start Me Up" if we sponsored the Rolling Stones next concert tour at a cost of $10 million, which I simply didn't have in my budget to spend. But, the Start Me Up concept was so strong and the idea so bold, it wouldn't have the same effect with any other song, so at the end of May 1995, I flew to Amsterdam to personally meet with key Stones personnel to try to negotiate a better deal.

The Stones were set to perform two "unplugged" concerts at the Paradiso, and I arrived the day before their back-to-back shows. I met with their concert organizer, as well as the litany of folks he brought with him, in a big, ornate conference room in an old, elegant European hotel. During our meeting, we could hear the Stones fans huddled outside hoping to catch a glimpse of the rock stars. We discussed the deal all day but didn't make any substantial progress. They asked me to stay the next day to discuss the deal more and attend the concert, but because I was slated to leave early the next morning, they invited me to the dress rehearsal that night.

It was fantastic. Unbelievable. I was one of only two people in the whole place who were not Stones personnel. They played for two or three hours, and they couldn't have sounded better. I could tell the band members were close; they would stop periodically to discuss something and joke around. Jagger gave Ron Wood a hard time about all the cigarettes he smoked. It was an epic evening, and when I was asked if I wanted to meet the Stones, I thought about it and then politely declined. It had been such a perfect night—my own private Rolling Stones concert—and I didn't want to ruin it. I'd met enough famous people during my time at Microsoft that I preferred to hold on to the perfection of the concert rather than risk tarnishing that. (I experience outrage from people about half the time when I tell them I could have met the Stones, while the other half think I was a genius to just end the night with the perfect concert.)

Negotiations continued over the phone for a good month after I went back to the States. They asked for certain rights or limitations on how we could use the music, and I countered. They asked for millions more than my budget allowed, and I told them we weren't even close and then offered something dramatically less that I thought was fair. I rolled the dice and gave my ad team permission to start moving forward with the commercial, assuming I could successfully complete the deal— though they were also working on a backup campaign.

As time rolled on, my team was appropriately apoplectic, as we were already well beyond the time we should have had the music. But some negotiations are a delicate dance, and this was one of them. So finally, when I thought the timing was right, I handed down my final offer and gave them 24 hours to agree, or I was going to go with our backup ads. They called the next day with the go-ahead. We signed the contract, and they sent us the recording of the song, it was incorporated into the ad, and the rest, as they say, is history.

Some have called the Start Me Up ad the most successful commercial Microsoft ever had. But overall, though extremely visible, the ad was a small part of the whole marketing effort, and the marketing effort was only a part of the mammoth effort that went into developing such an iconic, successful product. Microsoft sold 7 million copies of Windows 95 on diskettes and CDs in the first seven weeks, and within a year, 40 million. In 1995, 60 million computers were sold worldwide. Ten years later, that number surpassed 200 million, nearly all of them pre-installed with Windows 95.[2]

THE BUSINESS SUCCESS IMPERATIVE

Whether you are creating a company strategy like Bill Gates and Paul Allen did when they bet first on the PC, or later on GUI, or creating a marketing strategy like I did with Windows 95, it is imperative to get the strategy right and make the right bets. Nothing is more critical. If you get your strategy right, you have the best chance at success.

Now perhaps saying that creating a winning strategy is most important to the success of a business or a business leader isn't some deep new transformative insight. Even to me, it seems like common sense. But, despite having asked this question innumerable times at every strategy presentation I have given (to very smart and senior businesspeople and MBAs at topflight schools, I might add), strategy has yet to be mentioned by anyone in the audience. The audience even has a big hint. When I ask the question, a big fat title slide projected behind me displays the title of the talk with the word **STRATEGY** in huge bold letters.

The natural conclusion from this experience, supported by what I experienced at Microsoft and have seen with my consulting and my work as a member of numerous boards of directors with companies large and small, is that most businesspeople understand strategy is important, but they undervalue just how important it really is. If you are going to do one thing to help your business, your company, or your division in a large company—no matter what business you're in, no matter what country or countries in which you're competing—focus first on building a winning strategy. It is worth repeating: A winning strategy is the business success imperative. It is probably why, after countless speeches, no one has ever come up to me to dispute the importance or the preeminence of a winning strategy to business success. Once I talk about it, no one debates it.

But what the heck is strategy? Simply put, your strategy is your plan to compete. It's the bets you're making, your plan of attack to win and achieve your business goals. All companies make lots of bets every day, but most businesses have one fundamental bet (some businesses, generally larger, more diverse companies, have multiple fundamental bets). As I already discussed, Microsoft bet that the personal computer would be a success and then made a second bet on GUI, and then executed on both very well. Lotus and WordPerfect initially made the right bets and built excellent products, but they made critical strategy missteps by not betting on Windows and are now relegated to the history books. Marie Kondo bet everything that people cared a lot about tidying up.

Steve Ballmer, the longtime Microsoft CEO and owner of the National Basketball Association (NBA) Los Angeles Clippers, made a bold bet in 2019 to compete immediately for a championship by trading a record-setting collection of top draft choices and two excellent young players in exchange for all-star Paul George. With Paul George in hand, the Clippers were then able to persuade free agent (meaning he could sign with any team) Kawhi Leonard, another all-star and one of the best players in the NBA, to also sign with the team. Now with two marquee players and a strong squad to go with them, the Clippers should be in the championship hunt for many years to come.

Harlem Capital Partners is a minority-owned early-stage venture capital firm whose fundamental bet is on diversity-led startups with a goal to invest in 1,000 diverse founders over the next 20 years. Michelin is betting on building the highest-quality tires. Topper Fine Jewelers is a family-owned store in the San Francisco Bay Area that carries some of the best-known brands of premium watches and jewelry and is betting on a personal touch with its customers accompanied by a strong presence on social media sites like Instagram and Facebook.

Manini's is a food company betting on creating the best-tasting healthy flours, pasta, and bread products that are gluten-free. Seattle chef Edouardo Jordan, already a successful chef and restaurant owner with his contemporary American restaurant Salare, made a big bet that he could be successful with upscale authentic Southern cuisine; that bet has paid off as his second restaurant, JuneBaby, won the 2018 James Beard award for Best New Restaurant in the country, and Jordan himself won the prize for Best Chef: Northwest.

The Bill and Melinda Gates Foundation is betting that the path out of poverty begins when the next generation can access quality healthcare and a great education; the foundation's biggest bet is to globally increase access to healthcare and reduce infectious diseases and tackle the leading causes of child mortality. Though there is a long way to go, and progress is drastically different (and inequitable) in different parts of the world, progress is being made. The examples go on and on. Big or small, profit or nonprofit, companies you know and companies you have never heard of, no matter where you are in the world or what industry you're in, it all comes down to making the right fundamental bet. If you make the right bet, you still must do many other things right to be successful. But if you make the wrong bet, it doesn't matter what else you do; your business will fail. Like in poker, it helps to get a little luck along the way, but unlike in poker, in business you can't bluff your way to victory with a losing hand.

STRATEGY = E × mc²

So how do you decide what bet to place, what plan to make, and what strategy to pursue? To help figure that out, I created a formula that's based on Einstein's famous $E = mc^2$ equation. While his formula denotes the theory of special relativity, mine symbolizes what I call the strategic theory of relativity: Strategy = E × mc². Rather than a formula to determine what your strategy should be, Strategy = E × mc² is a way for you to think about and develop a winning strategy.

Customer value

There are three essential elements to the Strategy = E × mc² formula. The c stands for customer value; it's squared because it's the most important part of the equation. Sometimes, when used in the vernacular, value means price, but in my model, customer value is much broader. It is the worth or the usefulness of something—that is, the perceived benefits in comparison to what you paid.

In most businesses and most strategies, customer value is preeminent. Particularly in the early product development stages before you start selling a product, customer value can also be hard to judge; it's often subjective and reliant on understanding what customers perceive as valuable and how they view the competitors' offering compared to yours. You can do research, you can look at reviews and customer satisfaction, you can look at what's going on around the web and get feedback, or you could just rely on your instincts. Regardless of how you go about it, customer value is the most important part of most strategies.

With Windows 95, the results of beta testing were crucial in evaluating customer value, as was our research on what customers were looking for and our product designers' and developers' instinctive knowledge of what purposes the software needed to serve. The new version wasn't meant to be a flash in the pan or just a quick money maker; it was developed to make technology accessible for users and to provide cutting-edge functionality that would set the precedent for all operating systems that came after it.

Customer value can extend far beyond the typical exchange of tangible goods, though. For example, there's a company called LaborX that was started by Yscaira Jimenez, the youngest of five children in a Dominican immigrant family. She witnessed her older brother's struggle to land a stable living-wage job despite having an important skill set, which prompted her to pursue a career in education to help people like her brother graduate from high school and go on to find gainful employment. In 2018, she launched LaborX, an online talent marketplace that connects the nation's diverse and untapped workforce with innovative employers. In the company's own words, it's "The LinkedIn for the linked out."[3]

The value LaborX provides extends far beyond the people who are finding work; there's a case to be made for businesses everywhere. Studies have found that diverse teams—with gender, ethnic, and racial diversity—outperform more homogenous ones. Outperforming teams lead to companies that have higher financial returns, improved morale, and higher retention, all of which positively affect a company's bottom line.[4] Why not increase value for your customer by increasing the value and diversity of your people?

Market potential

The *m* stands for market potential. Market potential is ultimately about how much money you can make, how much profit. How do you find markets with a lot of profit? You look at market size. Sometimes a few people in a small market where you could charge a high price equals good market potential, but most of the time, you want a large market. That said, you want a large market with a true need for your product or service. A recent analysis of the top 20 reasons for startup failures noted that the number one reason is that startups were tackling problems that were interesting to solve rather than problems that served a market need, which was the case in 42 percent of the 101 cases reviewed.[5] Many other factors are important in judging market potential; for example, competition and reach. Even if you have a high market potential, you have to have a viable way to reach your customers.

Now, there are exceptions to every rule. Take WhatsApp, for example. WhatsApp is a free, cross-platform messaging mobile app that shows you can make a lot of money and have huge market potential without actually making any money at all. Facebook purchased it for $19 billion in 2014. If it's a free platform that doesn't even earn any revenue from advertisements, why did Facebook spend so much to buy it? Well, of course, because that's how much the app was worth to Facebook.[6]

Though I'm vastly oversimplifying, 450 million users at the time of purchase (over 2 billion users today),[7] growth opportunity, future prospects, behavioral data, the international credibility that WhatsApp had in Europe and developing countries where Facebook was weaker, contact lists, the strong mobile play in a mobile world, keeping the app out of the hands of competitors, eventual monetization . . . all of those things have a price tag.

In the tech sector in particular, sometimes market potential (at least in the short- and medium-term) is judged not by how much money you make, but by other things like the number of customers you have and how that volume can open the door for revenue and market expansion at some point in the future.

Execution

The *E* stands for execution. If strategy is your plan to compete, and execution helps you compete, then execution is a key part of strategy. That's important to remember. Ultimately, there are three types. The first is *strategic* execution. These are ways you can use execution as your core bet to compete directly with your competition—like sales, marketing, culture, and distribution. Often this happens when products are commodities or there is little customer value difference between products, à la Pepsi and Coke, or Old Spice and Axe. Old Spice actually makes for a really interesting case study on strategic execution.

Old Spice has been on the shelves since 1938 and was often

associated with older men; it seemed like every grandfather in the world used it as his signature scent. But all of that changed when Axe came to the United States in 2002 and turned the male grooming product industry on its head—instead of focusing on the effectiveness of their product as an odor blocker, Axe promoted themselves as the product to buy if you wanted to attract beautiful women. Old Spice, whose 2007 scent Glacial Falls was performing horribly and was in danger of being discontinued, hired an advertising agency and underwent a complete rebrand in the name of salvaging their product(s) and reputation.

Glacial Falls became Swagger—the scent that would transform nerdy wimps into strong, manly studs. The Old Spice Swagger campaign featured traditional print and television ads, which also made their way onto YouTube (the original ad, "The Man Your Man Could Smell Like," has more than 57 million views), as well as a hugely successful online campaign that gave guys the opportunity to "swaggerize" their online image. All aspects of the campaign showed off the brand's new look and attitude and completely revitalized the company, both in credibility and sales.

When the fundamental bet you're making is to out-execute your competition, that's when you know it's strategic execution. Often it's done through building a brand and using marketing to beat the competition, like the Old Spice example. Other times, it is done by trying to be the lowest-cost producer, like when brands such as Whirlpool strive for manufacturing efficiency. Sometimes it's done through distribution, as seen through the many companies today that have mastered the art of selling on Amazon. IBM was once known for having the best sales force. Execution is always a core part of strategy success, but with strategic execution, it is *the* core part, the fundamental bet to win.

The second type is *customer value* execution, or the ways that you actually use execution to curate the customer value—like through manufacturing or design. It's one thing to have a strategy that counts on unique customer value versus the competition, but the idea is only the first part of the equation. You have to execute successfully on that idea, and that's what customer value execution is all about.

The examples here are endless, because it fits almost everything you can think of where someone is trying to have a better product. The iPhone and AirPods would not be exceptional products without the thoughtful design and manufacturing that go into them. Tesla has had production challenges, but their product design has been terrific. Sonos has a strategy to have high-quality, easy-to-use wireless audio products, and their strategy only works if they actually execute on it by building great speakers and a great experience. *The New York Times* has a strategy to "seek the truth and help people understand the world" through high-quality media, but they have to execute on that, and most people, I think, would say they have.

It's important to note, however, that execution is never a one-and-done type of endeavor. Especially as it pertains to customer value, execution is as ongoing as strategy itself and requires constant assessment and iteration. A prime example (and cautionary tale) is J.Crew. The brand started in 1983 as a preppy catalogue-only company, turned into a dominant clothing chain with a brick-and-mortar presence by the early 1990s, and then lost steam around 1998. From then until 2003, three CEOs cycled through the fading brand. Then, Mickey Drexler, the ex-Gap CEO, invested $10 million of his own money into J.Crew in return for a 22 percent stake and the CEO title. Soon after he arrived, he discovered Jenna Lyons, who had been quietly working in the design department for over a decade. Together they began to nurture the brand, elevating the product through better design and better fabrics. Drexler and Lyons designed and executed a vision to build a brand that was synonymous with style and luxury, and at first, it worked: Total sales in 2003 were just short of $690 million, and by 2011, that figure soared to just under $2 billion.[8]

But by 2014, cracks started to show and sales began to fall. J.Crew went from a net income of $35.4 million to a reported loss of $607.8 million in one year.[9] Moody's Investors Service downgraded J.Crew due to a "declining earnings trend stemming from weak execution in a challenging apparel retail environment."[10] Consumers and critics alike expressed dismay over J.Crew's prices and the company's misunderstanding of its core audience. How did it all go so wrong?

The consensus was that the brand had executed poorly on its strategy of stylish basics and gone too far upscale and fashion forward for its customers. J.Crew also missed the ever-evolving consumer shopping trends (like e-commerce and the rise of athleisure, for example) and seemingly dismissed the lingering effects of the recession. They had a reputation for accessible high fashion, but slowly lost grasp of their accessibility and their fashion. In short: J.Crew's execution wasn't in sync with its strategy, and they weren't providing their customers with what they wanted. Customer value execution only works if you actually execute to curate customer value. Fast-forward to the present and J.Crew is still struggling to find its footing. In January of 2020, they hired former Victoria's Secret executive Jan Singer as CEO in an effort to turn things around.[11]

The third type is *financial* execution. This refers to the ways you build market potential and make money—standard, though not necessarily easy, stuff like accounting, managing costs, financial reporting, and so on. For businesses large and small, the financial environment is continuously changing, which makes the management and execution of those finances even more paramount. When this goes badly, people often have to come in to lead a turnaround, perform layoffs, or worse.

One such example is General Motors (GM), one of the world's most revered automakers that faced disaster in the late 2000s when it filed for bankruptcy and laid off tens of thousands of workers. The debt was the result of a Great Depression–esque economic downturn that translated to a loss of billions, and by the time the company closed its books on 2008, it was in the red by a staggering $30.9 billion.

Bankruptcy is often a killer of companies, and for a global company as big and complex as GM, a "normal" bankruptcy surely would have meant the end, but redemption came in the form of a federal government bailout. With the intent of preventing massive job losses and destabilizing damage to the entire manufacturing sector, an Obama-appointed team swept in with a way for GM to survive bankruptcy: Through a novel use of the bankruptcy code, they could save the company by segregating and spinning out its valuable assets, while Washington furnished billions in taxpayer funds to make sure the company was viable.[12]

In June 2009, GM filed for bankruptcy with $82 billion in assets and $173 billion in liabilities. It was the largest industrial bankruptcy in history, which makes it all the more extraordinary that just a year later, the company roared back to profitability. After trimming costs and killing its struggling Pontiac, Saturn, and Hummer divisions, GM went public again, raising roughly $20 billion. By the end of 2013, the government had sold off the last of its GM shares, recovered $39 billion of the $49.5 billion of taxpayer money the Treasury had invested into the GM bailout,[13] and capped a remarkable turnaround that saved an estimated 1.2 million jobs.[14]

35

It hasn't necessarily been smooth sailing for GM since its epic turnaround—faulty ignition switches led to major recalls that cost the company billions in victim compensation, repair costs, and other expenses over the course of a couple of years. Then in 2018, GM announced a major restructuring that would shut down production at five facilities in North America and reduce its salaried workforce by 15 percent in order to reinvest money into technology.[15]

Even though earnings were up and balance sheets were healthy prior to that announcement, sales were starting to slip in China and North America (two of GM's biggest and most important markets), so it's safe to say that GM was trying to get ahead of a potential crisis by making cuts sooner rather than later. And with a history of poor financial execution, it wasn't a bad idea. No one wants to botch financial execution twice.

There is a lot to consider when building a winning strategy. Just as no serious competitor should head onto the field without a game plan, no businessperson should step into the boardroom without one. The moving parts of a successful plan can be exponentially easier to develop if you use the Strategy = $E \times mc^2$ formula; by identifying and prioritizing customer value, market potential, and execution, a winning strategy can be methodically constructed.

Remember Marie Kondo? If we look at her company, KonMari Media, using the formula, we can see why her book turned into a movement and then an empire. For one, she provides customer value in spades. Her approach to "tidying up," known as the KonMari Method, isn't centered on throwing things away but figuring out what you want to keep based on whether or not it "sparks joy." That joy, in and of itself, creates immeasurable customer value for those who experience it, and imagine how much that multiplies as the decluttering principles are applied to other areas of followers' lives, like business, finances, relationships, and so on.

Second, the market potential is strong. KonMari's niche is a blend of self-help and self-care, both of which are large markets on their own, but since they're not always joined together, it gives KonMari a unique offering. In the age of excess in which we live, the need is clearly present. A key component of market potential is reach, and KonMari uses books, web, in-person consultations and seminars, and online streaming as viable ways to reach its customers.

Third, KonMari executes well—she has spread her method and grown her business through her own advocacy and via her network of consultants. Her marketing has carefully and thoughtfully cultivated a unique image and brand, and her products, like her books, are very well done. Put it all together, and she has built a tidy operation. (Sorry, I couldn't resist.)

Business success requires a winning strategy; there is no successful company that doesn't have one. And as we've covered, those strategies can and should be customized according to your specific business goals, which goes for all types of business and all types of roles—from an entrepreneur with a startup, to a divisional team member in a large company, to an executive who knows a strategy reset is needed.

So let's say you built a strategy. How do you know if it's a good one? Is there a way to poke holes in it before others do? How can you determine if the bet you're about to make will pay off? Or what if you are trying to build a strategy and don't know what to do? Stay with me.

CHAPTER 2

Scoring Your Strategy

Numbers are a super simple and illustrative way to compare how you are doing with others. As we all know, we want the highest credit score, the lowest golf score, the highest score in football or basketball games, and in the social media world in which we live, the most number of likes on our posts.

There is also a way to figure out and assign a score to the Strategy = $E \times mc^2$ equation. I call it the Strategy First Score (SFS). One benefit of using SFS with the $E \times mc^2$ model is that you can use it to calculate a score that gives an analytical and visual representation of how your strategy compares with that of your competitors. I like to use a 5-point scale and .5 increments (so you can give a score from 0.5 to 5). The 5-point scale not only provides simplicity, it also places customer value at the right level. Using say a 10-point scale tips the scales too much and over-weighs customer value versus market potential and execution since the customer value number is squared.

BRINGING SFS TO LIFE

To show the model in action, I'll use Apple as an example. Steve Jobs reset the Apple strategy completely around the year 2000. It went from being a computer company to being about consumer electronics and digital devices. It was a perfect reset because it took advantage of the core DNA of Apple, combining hardware and software into a compelling product. In 2001, Apple introduced the iPod and in 2003 the iTunes music store.

Jobs also recognized that the personal computer would no longer be at the center of a digital world. Instead, there would be many digital devices, and the personal computer was just one of those. Jobs realized (or he got lucky) that cellular data speeds were about to be faster than ever before, making it possible for smartphones to do some very interesting things other than voice calls and text messages. Interestingly enough, Jobs' revelations and the smartphone project that ensued occurred because of an interaction between Jobs and a guy from Microsoft whom he hated. According to Scott Forstall, the iPhone's co-inventor, the Microsoft employee was the spouse of a friend of Laurene Powell Jobs, Steve's wife, and "anytime [Steve] had any kind of social interaction with that guy, he'd come back pissed off."[1]

The social interaction in question included a conversation where the

Microsoft employee told Jobs that his employer had "solved computing" with its Tablet PC effort. Like the tablets that would come later, the Tablet PCs were smaller and lighter than laptop computers and included touch displays, but the tablets Microsoft was building required customers to use a stylus. Jobs was not a fan of styluses, a fact he wasn't shy about. Jobs said that users were always losing styluses and that they were cumbersome. In addition, Forstall, dramatically retelling the story, said Jobs, referring to his fingers, exclaimed, "They're idiots, you don't use a stylus, you're born with ten of them!" Jobs also did not like the "resistive" touch screens in use at that time that required users to push down hard and deform the screen. So an infuriated Jobs told his team, "Let's show him how it's really done," and he kicked off a project at Apple to outdo Microsoft, developing a touch screen device with passive touch and multi-touch that would rely on fingers, not a stylus.

The initial development effort focused on building a tablet. But soon after, Jobs and Forstall were having lunch and saw people sitting there using their cell phones, though none seemed to be happy about it. To Jobs, that was an opportunity, especially since folks at Apple were concerned that eventually phones might replace iPods. So Jobs asked Forstall if Apple could shrink the multi-touch project down to a phone-size display, and once early prototypes came to fruition, it was clear the team was on to something big. The iPhone, one of the most important products in tech history, was born.

As the iPhone origin story shows, taking advantage of societal and technological trends with a stellar product was where Jobs and his team at Apple really excelled. After two and a half years of development, Apple introduced the iPhone in June 2007, the subsequent iPhone 3G a year later, and the iPhone 3GS a year after that. The iPhone wasn't the first smartphone by any means, but all three versions were megahits because they were dramatically better products than the other smartphones on the market.

To name just a few of its key innovations, the iPhone pioneered an easy-to-use multi-touch screen interface that let the iPhone smoothly pinch-to-zoom. It also had multitasking, excellent hardware, and sensors that automatically rotated the screen horizontally or vertically to match the device orientation. Those features, and many others, blew away the smartphones of competitors like BlackBerry, Motorola, Nokia, and Samsung. With the iPhone 3G and iOS2 (the software that runs the iPhone behind the scenes), Apple introduced the App Store, which then helped the iPhone grow further in popularity and profitability via third-party apps.

The iPhone is a great example of how we can use $E \times mc^2$ to bring strategy to life and calculate an SFS. Let's build this visually over the next few pages. On execution, I'd give Nokia and BlackBerry a 3 and Apple a 4.

Apple iPhone 2001-2009

Nokia/Blackberry 3

Apple 4

Execution

When Nokia and BlackBerry initially released their "smartphones"—the Nokia 9000 Communicator in 1996 and the BlackBerry 5810 in 2002—they were smash hits. (In fact, in the fourth quarter of 2006, the year before the iPhone was announced, there were 22 million smartphones sold worldwide, of which Nokia was the market leader accounting for 50 percent of all shipments, and Researcher In Motion (RIM), the BlackBerry maker, was second in share.[2]) But when Apple released its iconic smartphone in 2007, it made the all other phones in the industry look obsolete.

We could go round and round about the execution flaws of the Nokia and RIM when they were faced with such competition, but it ultimately came down to Nokia being an engineering company that needed more customer and marketing savvy (though perhaps it would be more accurate to say that Nokia was a hardware company rather than a software company), and BlackBerry failing to anticipate that consumers—not business customers—would drive the smartphone revolution. Neither company was particularly agile, and both ultimately failed to execute a successful strategy in the face of a rapidly transforming industry.

Though there were some early hiccups with the speed and reliability of AT&T's cellular network, the overall execution of the iPhone rollout was solid, and Jobs's marketing was superb. The Macworld Expo was Apple's annual tradeshow dedicated to the Apple Macintosh platform and renowned for Steve Jobs's keynote addresses. In 1998, he introduced the iMac, in 2001 the iPod, and in 2007 he gave the world the iPhone. The perfectly executed sales pitch of the iPhone (in which he checked Apple's stock using the phone and it had gone up more than $2.50 in one hour; by the end of the day, the company's value had risen 8.3 percent, while RIM, the creators of the BlackBerry, watched its stock fall

7.9 percent[3]) was accompanied by handpicked follow-up interviews and a commercial that featured a succession of movie clips of characters answering telephones and saying hello. There was an intentional mystique, an air of secrecy around Apple, and what surrounded the release of its newest product was no different. As a reporter for the *Globe* said in the months before the iPhone hit stores, "I can't think of any other company so able to co-opt journalism for its marketing campaign." I might argue that Windows 95 set the standard, but I'm of course biased.

In addition to superior marketing, Apple product execution was better than the competition. Before the iPhone, network providers like AT&T and Verizon had a tendency to add their own functionality or request the features they wanted from the cell phone manufacturers, and often these changes were not well received by customers. The exclusive partnership Apple had with AT&T allowed Apple to control the product so the company could achieve the user experience it wanted.

On market potential, all three companies earn high scores because cell phones and smartphones were such large and rapidly growing markets—they're like Mount Everest in scale. I'd assign Apple a 5 and the others a 4.

Apple iPhone 2007-2009

Nokia/Blackberry

Apple

■ *Execution*   ▨ *Market Potential*

Apple gets a larger number because it only sold smartphones, the most profitable and fastest-growing type of phone, whereas Nokia and BlackBerry sold a slew of other types of phones, from car phones to flip phones to "email-capable mobile phones." Additionally, Apple earned revenue from the sale of applications via the App Store, not to mention the Apple Stores themselves, which were an important innovation that launched several years before the iPhone. The company not only ensured distribution and promotion for Apple products, but it also reinforced the hip, forward-thinking image Apple was trying to convey.

As far as customer value, Apple dominated the competition for all the reasons already stated: quality, ease of use, cutting-edge technology, and exclusivity. Of course, customer value of a product is not the same for every customer, so when determining your customer value score, you have to take an average or generalize. In Apple's case though, it clearly earned a strong score. I'd give Apple a 4 and Nokia and Black-Berry a 2.5.

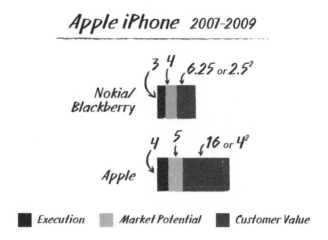

In the end, you get a pretty amazing difference in SFSs. Completing the math places Apple's score over four times the competition's: 320 for the Apple iPhone and 75 for Nokia and BlackBerry.

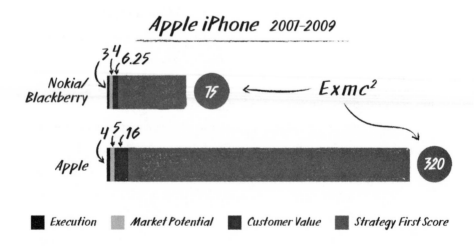

Apple blew everyone away during the early years of the iPhone because it far outcompeted the other smartphone companies on both customer value and execution, and a numerical use of the model really brings that home. An SFS over four times the competition in a large market means, in the words of my sons, "You'll make bank." If we fast-forward to present day and look at the smartphone market, we can see that it's grown exponentially. But not surprisingly, Apple's success attracted many competitors, and now, with the passage of time, competitors have closed the huge feature gap that Apple had with the first few iPhones.

IT'S ALL RELATIVE

While few would debate the preeminence of the iPhone in the early years, a healthy debate could be held about who makes the best phones today. Some people prefer the iPhone, but others prefer phones from other manufacturers like Samsung. The iPhone 11 Pro and 11 Pro Max and the Samsung Galaxy S10+ are similarly equipped phones with similar hardware specs. Each has some advantages over the other and, of course, each has a unique user experience. And more than likely, that same dynamic will be true even if newer models have come out between now and when you are reading this book.

Yes, the smartphone market has become a horse race. All the companies, including Apple, are struggling to develop unique breakthrough innovations that would give them the same dramatic advantages the original iPhones had; everyone is trying to find ways to create a huge leg up on the competition. With each new major smartphone introduction, each company catches up on some features and inches ahead on a few others. So even though the current iPhone is way better than the original iPhone, its market position, while still very strong, is not as dominant.

The worldwide smartphone unit market share leader as of 2018 and the first half of 2019 is not Apple but Samsung, with about 20 percent market share.[4] Apple and Huawei, a Chinese multinational telecommunications and consumer electronics company, go back and forth for second and third. Oppo, Xiaomi, and Vivo (three other Chinese smartphone makers) have also gained share and, when combined with Huawei, make up about one-third of smartphone unit sales.[5] In terms of the operating systems running the phones themselves, Google, as the creator of the Android operating system that powers almost all non-Apple phones, has a dominating 85 percent share with Apple's iOS basically taking up the rest of the market.

Yet another consequence of the challenge smartphone makers have in developing new breakthrough innovations is that now, more than ever, they are also competing against themselves. The installed base of quality smartphones and the increase in the prices of current new phones combine to make it less compelling for current users to upgrade and buy new phones. The first quarter of 2019 was the sixth consecutive quarter of year-over-year sales declines for the global smartphone market.[6] According to BayStreet Research, a firm that tracks smartphone sales, back in 2015, iPhones were being replaced on average around every two years—of course, that was when most major carriers offered a "new every two" model that encouraged users to upgrade more regularly. Now, on average, new phone upgrades occur roughly every three years, and that period may continue to grow.[7] (Brian X. Chen, the lead consumer technology writer for *The New York Times*, reviewed the iPhone 11 and told his readers that older smartphone models are so good, customers should only definitely upgrade to one of the iPhone 11 models if their current device is at least five years old.[8]) To respond to this marketplace shift, Apple is shifting its strategy by putting a greater emphasis on selling hardware that adds value to the iPhone like the AirPods and services that generate ongoing revenue like Apple Music, the App Store, Apple Pay, and iCloud. In 2018 alone, the App Store generated $50 billion in sales, and Apple gets a nice slice of that, or I guess I could also say a nice bite—about 30 percent, a cool $15 billion.[9]

It's clear that Apple still has a leadership position. As of 2019, it brings in more profit than any other company in the smartphone market and is the US market share leader. One reason for that is that Apple targets the higher-end, more profitable segment of the smartphone market. Another is that Apple generates more profit from the sales of apps than other phone manufacturers, both because iPhone users buy more apps for their phones in the first place and because companies like Samsung share app revenue, not only with the app developer (as does Apple) but with Google, the creator of the Play Store on the Android phone operating system. Plus, Apple has a business model advantage with its own brick-and-mortar stores, because owning the store gives Apple higher margins. Samsung and other smartphone manufacturers primarily sell through third parties.

Strategy First Score Comparisons:
Apple iPhone vs Competition

	Samsung 2019	Apple 2019	Nokia/Blackberry 2007–2009	Apple 2007–2009
Execution	4	4.5	3	4
Market Potential	4.5	5	4	5
Customer Value	4	4.5	2.5	4
Strategy Fist Score $(E \times mc^2)$	288	456	75	320

A look at the SFS of the current iPhone versus Samsung reflects the changes that have happened since the first few years of iPhone dominance that we discussed and was shown on the charts in the previous pages. As the table shows, Apple has gone from a score of over four times the competition to a score that is about 1.6 times the competition, and one could easily argue that I was not generous enough with the scores I gave Samsung. With that said, the possible disparities in the precision of high and low scores doesn't really matter. This is all about getting a sense of how they compete *relative* to each other. And there's the key insight: It's all relative, and that's why Strategy = E × mc² is called the Strategic Theory of Relativity instead of just the Strategic Theory. The success of your strategy depends not on the quality of your strategy independently but on the quality of your strategy relative to your competition's strategy.

It's also important to reinforce that SFSs are not scientific; exact scores are not even possible to calculate. SFSs are dramatic simplifications that help you sense how your strategy compares to that of your competition. If you use reasonable and consistent assumptions, the scores will simply gauge the relative difference in the effectiveness of your strategy; having that frame of reference lets you consider where your strategy is working against the competition and where it isn't.

That reasoning applies to every product in every market. Do you have a favorite soda between Coke and Pepsi? I recently did a blind taste test of several different sodas at a presentation I gave at a major Fortune 500 company, and no one guessed all of them right. Coca-Cola products versus Pepsi, diet and regular, it didn't matter. It turns out, and independent research validates this,[10] most people can't tell the difference. So why do people choose the soda they choose, especially if they can't even distinguish its difference in taste? Most people are loyal to whatever they drink because, often, they associate the brand with certain memories or experiences.

In a 2004 study, Pepsi and Coca-Cola were blindly given to participants, who gave similar responses in regards to taste. However, when the drinks were labeled, participants displayed a preference for Coca-Cola.[11] Maybe they remember their grandpa always had a six-pack of it in his fridge, or they identify consciously or subconsciously with Coca-Cola's advertising campaigns, or they have an aversion to Pepsi based on that one night when they mixed it with too much rum. You can't win 'em all; so win what you can. How? You can use the model to think about how best to compete. In the case of Coke versus Pepsi, if the companies can't compete on customer value (taste), then they have to compete on execution (in this case, marketing and image-building is key, as are other things such as distribution).

The same dynamic is in play with Old Spice and Axe. In regards to your own endeavors, if you can't compete on customer value, perhaps because you have a commodity product like cola, then you have to compete on strategic execution, in this case, marketing and advertising.

In 2006, sales of imported beer began to dip as craft beer became more and more popular in the United States. Dos Equis, owned by Amsterdam-based brewer Heineken, was one of the imported beers that saw declining sales, especially when pitted against its similar tasting competitors Coors, Budweiser, and Miller Lite. Knowing it had to do something drastic to differentiate itself, Dos Equis upped its advertising game and launched "The Most Interesting Man in the World" campaign—commercials that featured an older bearded, debonair gentleman who found himself in outrageous situations like surfing a killer whale, slamming a revolving door, and finding the Fountain of Youth, but not taking a drink because he "wasn't thirsty." Every ad included the tagline, "I don't always drink beer, but when I do, I prefer Dos Equis," with the sign-off, "Stay thirsty, my friends."

Dos Equis sales began to rise significantly—in the first two years of the campaign, its sales rose more than 22 percent, while imported beer sales on the whole dropped 11 percent[12]—but the more important reason the campaign was so remarkable was because it took a polar opposite approach than that of every other beer brand. While Budweiser was making ads directed toward young guys who like to party, Dos Equis opted to feature a Hemingway-esque worldly figure that consumers could aspire to be. Though that's not to say that their ads lacked a sense of humor.

On the contrary, I could recount the commercials' witty one-liners about The Man for days:

"His blood smells like cologne."

"Once a rattlesnake bit him, after five days of excruciating pain, the snake finally died."

"He can speak Russian . . . in French."

"He gave his father 'the talk.'"

"If he were to punch you in the face, you would have to fight off a strong urge to thank him."

"Mosquitoes refuse to bite him purely out of respect."

"He lives vicariously through himself."

The clever advertising created a cult-like obsession with The Man—evident through seemingly endless Halloween costumes, memes, and skits on *Saturday Night Live*—and catapulted a relatively small brand into the minds of beer drinkers. Sales tripled during the campaign's nine-year run, and in just the final year the ads aired (2016), sales of Dos Equis Lager Especial grew 10.2 percent, to $325.3 million.[13] Those are shockingly high numbers for any beer, and even more so when you consider the poor state of mass-market beer against craft brewed beers.

Of course, it's impossible to say how much of this sales increase can be directly attributed to the campaign—sales figures are only a rough gauge of a campaign's effectiveness. But the point is that Dos Equis intentionally compensated when it appeared they couldn't properly compete on customer value or market potential—they put their eggs in the strategic execution basket.

You can't win 'em all; so win what you can, remember? Using the model to think about how best to compete often means mixing and matching, weighing and shifting, and compensating and counteracting the different components within the equation.

Allow me to stress that key point again: No one should compete in only one area. You try to have a fundamental bet, like Apple did with the experience of the iPhone, or Tesla with electric cars, or Microsoft with GUI. But even with that bet, you still want to outmaneuver your competition everywhere you can. The more places you gain an advantage over the competition, the better chance you have at achieving superior results. From a Strategy = E × mc^2 model perspective, it gives you a higher SFS via a higher customer value, market potential, and execution scores.

The competition within the luxury car market is another industry where we can show the relative difference in the effectiveness of strategy. Though certainly cars don't compete strictly with the other cars in their designated segment, the BMW 7 Series, Mercedes S-Class, and Tesla Model S, in auto industry terminology, are all considered large luxury vehicles, so here is an SFS analysis comparing them (though for the purpose of simplicity when assigning scores, I'm going to combine the BMW and Mercedes as one entity and pit it against Tesla). For execution, I would give both BMW and Mercedes a 4. But Tesla is another story. On one hand, they have been innovative in important areas. For example, the company eliminated the whole car dealership model. Tesla has some service centers and showrooms, but if you want to buy a car, you simply do so online, directly from Tesla on their website.

That reduces costs and hassle for consumers. On the other hand, the company has faced production problems, has delivered products late, and has some quality control issues. So, to be conservative, I would give Tesla a 3.5 for execution.

Large Luxury Cars 2019

You may want to argue with me about that, but again, this is less about the numbers and more about how these companies compete relative to each other. For market potential, Tesla comes in with a similar score to BMW and Mercedes—I gave them both a 3.5 because the large luxury car market is not a large one by car standards (since cars in this segment are expensive).

Large Luxury Cars 2019

BMW/
Mercedes

4 3.5

Tesla

3.5 3.5

■ Execution   ▨ Market Potential

But customer value—remember, the most important part of the equation, which is why it's squared—is where Tesla really pulls ahead.

The Tesla is not only electric, which is a unique and compelling difference in and of itself, but it also has other significant innovations like automatic software updates, autopilot features, and improved weight distribution and battery performance. What's more, they offer customers a nationwide network of charging stations. Historically, charging stations have been unreliable in that third-party options were sparse and companies often went bankrupt. Tesla included charging in its strategy to make the foreign concept of driving electric much more accessible. Another key Tesla advantage is that it requires less service than traditional cars. Tesla cars are basically a chassis, one or more electric motors, a huge battery, and some very smart software. There is no complicated engine to tune or oil to change, no transmission, radiator, spark plugs, or emissions control hardware, and so on. No other car manufacturers offer customers this range of feature and sustainability options, and this gives Tesla an edge. As a consequence, I gave Tesla a 4.5, and BMW and Mercedes, who have solid cars, each got a 4 for customer value.

Large Luxury Cars 2019

$$4 \overset{3.5}{\downarrow} 16 \text{ or } 4^2$$

BMW/
Mercedes

$$3.5 \overset{3.5}{\downarrow} 20.25 \text{ or } 4.5^2$$

Tesla

■ Execution   ■ Market Potential   ■ Customer Value

Like I said, if one element of the equation comes in lower than the competition, you can make up for it in one of the other categories. Tesla's execution has been lower than the competition, but customer value was higher, so it ended up with a slightly higher score (248 compared to 224).

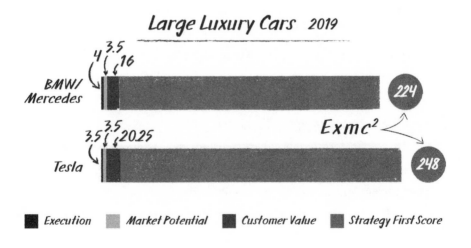

Large Luxury Cars 2019

BMW/
Mercedes
$$4 \overset{3.5}{\downarrow} 16$$
224

$$Exmc^2$$

Tesla
$$3.5 \overset{3.5}{\downarrow} 20.25$$
248

■ Execution   ■ Market Potential   ■ Customer Value   ■ Strategy First Score

The sales from this category reflect that. If you look at BMW (BMW 7 series) and Mercedes (Mercedes-Benz S-Class) US sales from the first half of 2019, they were both behind Tesla (Mercedes was number two and BMW number three).[14]

And it was much of the same in the first half of 2019 with US midsize luxury cars—the Tesla Model 3 sold nearly as many cars as its top three competitors (Lexus ES, BMW 5 series, and Mercedes E/CLS Class) combined.[15] The Tesla Model 3 also competes with the BMW 3 series and the Audi A4. The Tesla Model 3 did well in that space as well. It came in 13th in the overall US car market, and no other premium-class car even made the top 20.[16]

Now to be fair, Tesla is not yet a consistent money maker,[17] and other car manufacturers are adding or improving their electric cars. Some are even making completely different bets. For example, Toyota, Honda, and Hyundai are experimenting with zero-emissions vehicles using hydrogen fuel cell technology, shipping those cars today in limited quantities and locations. And that is the key lesson here. Tesla's fate will be based on its ability to improve execution, improve profitability, stay ahead of other car manufacturers, and grow market potential through new car models that reach more customers, such as the Model Y (a crossover due to ship in late 2020). But the competition will not make that journey easy. It is worth restating: strategy effectiveness, like so many things in life, is relative.

That consideration is where scoring your strategy will come in handy. Using the Strategy = $E \times mc^2$ model and assigning an SFS to your current strategy and that of your competitors will provide insight and help you think about what bets to make and how best you can compete. Take note of where your strategy falls short of your competitors' and adjust accordingly—a successful strategy is one that considers all the crucial components.

PART II

ACTIVATING THE
KEY STRATEGY
ELEMENTS

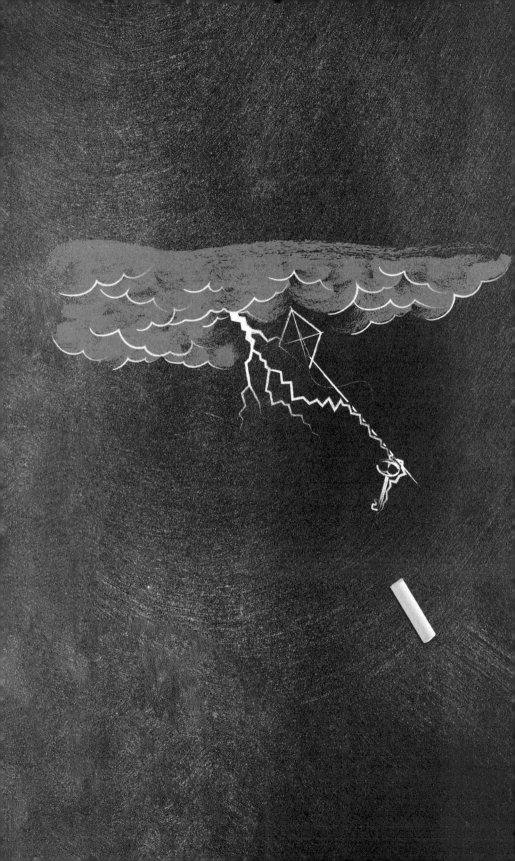

CHAPTER 3

Seek Change

Think for a moment about electricity. Many famous people contributed to its development. In 1752, Benjamin Franklin conducted his experiment with a kite, a key, and a storm that proved lightning and electric sparks were the same thing. Italian physicist Alessandro Volta discovered that particular chemical reactions could produce electricity, and in 1800, he constructed an early electric battery (the term *battery*, referring to an electrical cell, was coined by Franklin). In 1831, Michael Faraday created a crude power generator. Thomas Edison (and simultaneously British scientist Joseph Swan) invented the incandescent filament light bulb, the first practical light bulb that would light for hours, around 1878.

Later in the 1800s and early 1900s, engineer and inventor Nikola Tesla contributed to the birth of commercial electricity. George Westinghouse bought Tesla's patented motor for AC (alternating current), which led to further commercial development of electricity and AC winning "the war of currents" over DC (direct current).

How do you find winning strategies that help you maximize $E \times mc^2$ relative to the competition? The first way is to seek change. The invention of electricity, how it evolved, and the innovations that came about because of it, changed the world and created endless opportunities over time that continue today. Think about the growth of alternative energy and LED light bulbs and improved batteries. Change, if you'll pardon the pun, is often electrifying and usually difficult to manage, but whenever there's change, there's strategic opportunity. We've seen it time and time again.

Though there are numerous types of change you can seek, there are five types that I cover here, and each differentiates customer value through various means:

1. Technology

2. Innovation

3. New business models

4. Societal trends

5. New markets

TECHNOLOGY

The first is technology. While technology change comes in many forms, it is worth focusing on the internet because it has completely transformed business by providing new opportunities to reach customers, new ways to communicate, new ways to collaborate, new ways to advertise, new methods to provide customer service, new types of products, new ways to sell products, and so on and so on. OpenTable, Dell, Expedia, 23andMe, YouTube, Spotify, Skype, Twitter, Salesforce, Warby Parker, and Dollar Shave Club are just a few of the almost infinite examples of companies that have benefited from a strategy based on technology change.

Warby Parker is an online retailer of prescription eyeglasses and sunglasses. The company was launched in 2010 by two MBA students from the University of Pennsylvania after one of them lost a $700 pair of glasses and couldn't afford to replace them. He spent the first semester of grad school without glasses, squinting and complaining, until he and his friend dreamed up a business idea where they could undercut the sale of glasses by hundreds of dollars and sell them online rather than in physical stores.

Most people don't realize when they walk into a LensCrafters or Sunglass Hut that while there are 50 different brands of glasses, they're all owned and produced by one company who also happens to own the physical store the customer is standing in and the vision plan they used to pay for the glasses. The eyewear industry is dominated by that single company—Luxottica is its name—and they've been able to keep prices artificially high while reaping huge profits from consumers who have few other options. Why had no one questioned it before? Why was that the only way to design, manufacture, and sell glasses to people?

The founders of Warby Parker decided to circumvent traditional channels by designing glasses in-house and producing them under their own brand, thereby eliminating all unnecessary licensing fees, selling them directly to consumers without any wholesale or any kind of middleman. This allowed them to cut unnecessary markups, and leverage e-commerce by selling their products solely online.

Knowing people wanted to be able to try on glasses before purchasing them, Warby Parker launched a Home Try-On program where people could select five frames through their website and get them shipped free of cost. They then built upon that by using the camera capabilities of the iPhone so customers could try on virtual frames through augmented reality, a technology that overlaps computer-generated images (frames) onto real-world images (faces).[1]

Since the beginning, Warby Parker used technology to streamline the customer experience, thus creating one opportunity after another. Almost a decade since its inception, Warby Parker is now a $1 billion-plus brand that's sold millions of pairs of glasses in the United States. And not surprisingly, their success has led to the emergence of a lot of competitors. From well-known brands like Tom Ford and Burberry to newcomers like Cubitts and Ace & Tate, online optical shops have become the new normal.

It was the same type of story for Dollar Shave Club. You may have heard of the razor-razorblade business model. It refers to a business model where the core product is sold very inexpensively (the razor) and the disposable product that goes with it is sold for a high margin (the blade). In 2011, a guy named Michael Dubin was frustrated with that model. For one, razors, and razor blades in particular, were really expensive for what you got. And to buy them, you had to make a trip to the store, find the locked razor fortress, and then locate an elusive employee who had the key. Dubin figured there had to be a cheaper and more convenient way to get shaving supplies. He launched a beta site from his apartment where people could buy a razor for as little as one dollar plus shipping, and it would be sent to their doorstep. By 2012, he had funneled the early dollars from the beta phase into the production of a YouTube commercial that went viral and put his company on the map.

When Dubin started, the razor market was dominated by Gillette, which claimed 72 percent of the US market and had been purchased by Procter & Gamble (P&G) for $57 billion in 2005. Schick was a distant second. By 2015, four years after Dubin began, web sales for men's shaving gear had more than doubled industry-wide, to $263 million. The following year, Dollar Shave Club was the number one online razor company, with 51 percent of the market, compared with Gillette's 21.2 percent. It clearly spooked the industry giant who soon launched its own Gillette Shave Club and bought promoted tweets to claim things like "two million guys and counting no longer buy from the other shave clubs."[2] But Dubin's company kept growing, more than doubling its revenue every year since launching. It started with $6 million in 2012, earned a total of $163.5 million in 2015, and topped $250 million in sales in 2017.

Here's what was so ingenious about Dubin's concept: The traditional promotion and distribution model, used by P&G and others, costs a lot of money to cover research and development, television advertising, and retailer margins. Capitalizing on technology allowed Dubin to lower prices, deliver quality products to consumers, and eliminate the need for additional costs that come with wholesalers and retailers. And by using social media platforms like YouTube and Facebook, Dollar Shave Club was able to reach a market of 20 million people at a much lower cost than traditional media advertising.

But as was the case with Warby Parker, there were plenty of competitors who wanted in on Dollar Shave Club's unique model. Harry's is a similar company in that they deliver razors to your door, although their version of seeking change through technology came in the form of purchasing a razor factory in Germany in an effort to gain control of the entire process, including manufacturing their products. Another shaving subscription service, Billie, caters to women specifically. For their technological offering, they encase their blades in 360 degrees of charcoal shave soap, along with rounded edges to help women navigate curves.

Dollar Shave Club has since morphed into a subscription-based grooming brand that includes deodorant, skin care, cologne, and hair products and was acquired by P&G archrival Unilever for $1 billion in 2016.[3] Edgewell, owner of the Schick and Wilkinson razor brand acquired Harry's for $1.37 billion in 2019.[4] Warby Parker now has over 100 retail stores, more than 1,400 employees, and has provided over five million pairs of glasses to visually impaired people in over 50 countries through their Buy a Pair, Give a Pair program.[5] Both Warby Parker and Dollar Shave Club sought change by using web technology to reach customers and disrupt industries that erred on the side of more traditional marketing and distribution models. What would happen if you leveraged the ever-changing technology that is available?

INNOVATION

A second type of change you can seek is through innovation, which makes perfect sense since the word "innovate" is defined as making changes to something established. There is very little that could offer you more strategic advantage than innovation. Successful companies like Pixar, Nest, Tesla, Nespresso, Post-it, Bausch + Lomb, Prilosec OTC, Dyson, and Amazon Web Services show us just how much customer value new innovations provide.

In 2000, Amazon was a far different company than it is today—it was an e-commerce company struggling with scale problems. Those issues forced the company to build some solid internal systems to deal with their hyper-fast growth, and those systems laid the foundation for what would become Amazon Web Services (AWS).

In the early 2000s, Amazon built an e-commerce service called Merchant.com to help third-party merchants like Target and Marks & Spencer build online shopping sites. But, because Amazon had moved very quickly over the years in building out its technology platform, many components had become tangled together. Decoupling these individual pieces, or services, from each other turned out to be more painful and time-consuming than the fast-growing startup had ever imagined. The code was not easily shared between sites or easy to build on and customize.

At that point, the company took its first step toward building the AWS business by untangling that mess into a set of well-documented application programming interfaces (APIs), which solved some of the architecture problems. APIs provide an easy way for a developer of one program to access the capabilities of another program. A simple example is that when you print a document, the program you are using is "calling" the print APIs in whatever operating system you are using, such as Windows. While having a set of well-documented APIs drove the smoother development of Merchant.com, it also served the internal Amazon developer audience, and it set the stage for a much more organized and disciplined way of developing tools internally going forward.[6]

"We expected all the teams internally from that point on to build in a decoupled, API-access fashion, and then all of the internal teams inside of Amazon expected to be able to consume their peer internal development team services in that way," said Andy Jassy, the CEO of AWS. What this meant was that very quietly, around 2000, Amazon became a services company with no real fanfare.

But Amazon still had one major internal development challenge. Every time the company wanted to build a new application, it took too long because each team had to build its own infrastructure services, like the database, compute, and storage. Think of these services as the core foundation needed to run a website or web application. For example, all the product info you see when you go to buy a product from Amazon is pulled from a database, and all that info and more requires storage, just like a hard drive on a computer.

So Amazon realized two things: First, it could build a common set of services for its own use, and second, it also had a great business idea providing those same infrastructure services to developers and companies building applications. The advantages to developers was huge— they wouldn't have to spend time building the basic core services themselves; they could just get them from Amazon, which meant websites and applications could be built faster. Buying the services from Amazon was also less expensive, as even a small website could take advantage of Amazon's scale to get low pricing and not have to worry about difficult issues like how many servers to buy or the cost and headaches of network maintenance (which Amazon handles for the services it provides). Developers would also reduce IT (information technology) costs by reducing the size of their datacenter or even eliminating it altogether. There would also be far more flexibility. Need more storage for your website? Just order more from Amazon, and the company would provide it for you in a flash.

AWS was the first to market with a modern cloud infrastructure service when it launched Amazon Simple Storage Service (S3) in March 2006. As of the second quarter of 2019, AWS grew into the most successful cloud infrastructure company on the planet, garnering about one-third of the market. That's more than its four closest rivals—Microsoft, Google, Alibaba, and Tencent—combined, and by a fair margin. It is noteworthy, however, that competition in the market is increasing. Though Amazon is protesting the result, Microsoft was awarded a major $10 billion, ten-year cloud computer contract from the Department of Defense in October 2019. Overall, Microsoft's revenue and market share has grown materially over the last few years, and the company is the second leading player in the space. Amazon and Microsoft account for over half of all the money spent on cloud infrastructure services, which is impressive for such a high-growth, strategically important market.[7] But overall, Amazon has continued its leadership. Where once on-premise computing was the way to go, AWS opened the door to scalable, on-demand, metered services and fundamentally changed the way IT and web development operates. Today, AWS has a remarkable $33 billion annual sales runrate[8] and is the provider relied on by brand names like Pinterest, Slack, Airbnb, GE, Intuit, Goldman Sachs, and even the CIA.

When seeking to solve a recurring need, innovation can often be the smartest solution. In this case, it emerged organically out of the company's frustration with its inability to launch new projects, support customers, and deploy faster technology. AWS sought change, and when they couldn't find an already-established way forward that met their needs, AWS pioneered one. The same could be said for other advancements like 3-D printers, self-driving cars, voice recognition, and Blockchain (the robust technology underlying Bitcoin that, since its launch in 2009, no one has been able to counterfeit). These innovations have significantly influenced the business and consumer spheres, and products and capabilities beyond the wildest dreams of innovators just a decade ago are now commonplace realities.

NEW BUSINESS MODELS

The third type of change to consider when seeking customer value is new a business model. Companies like Redfin, IKEA, Uber, StubHub, Airbnb, Starbucks, Southwest Airlines, Paperless Post, and Costco have shown us how thinking outside the box when it comes to business models can create unique compelling advantages for customers, impel exponential growth, and create significant players in a variety of markets.

Costco is one of the world's top three retailers and the world's largest membership warehouse chain, and it's thrived by turning convention on its head. The members-only warehouse club was the brainchild of Sol Price, who introduced the groundbreaking retail concept in San Diego, California, in the mid-1970s in an airplane hangar. At that time, small business owners had no options other than to buy their products and supplies from regional wholesalers or cash-and-carry operations. Price set out to offer an alternative and created a business model that hadn't existed until then.

The concept was simple: Offer a small selection of products covering a broad range of goods and sell in bulk in order to keep prices low, usually at no more than a 10 percent markup over the wholesale cost. To maintain such discount prices, overhead was kept to a bare minimum. Products were stocked directly on the selling floor in minimally decorated warehouses built on cheap industrial land, sales help was almost nonexistent, and there would be no advertising, except to announce the opening of new stores. Selection was limited, offering the broad range but not the depth—and consequent inventory burden—of the typical department store. Products were bought in bulk directly from the manufacturers. Low margins were further offset by rapid inventory turnover, as high as 20 turns a year, allowing stores to pay suppliers quickly and achieve added early-payment discounts.[9] In exchange for getting goods at prices only slightly higher than wholesale, consumers purchased a membership for an annual fee, which, to this day, is revenue that's almost entirely profit.

Price Club transformed the retail world, and like with any good idea, others soon jumped on the bandwagon. In 1983, Price was faced with new competitors who successfully copied the Price Club idea: Wal-Mart's Sam's Clubs, Kmart's PACE Membership Warehouse, and Costco, whose Seattle, Washington-based Costco Wholesale Clubs (co-founded by Jeff Brotman and James Sinegal, the latter a protégé of Sol Price) directly challenged Price's hold on the West Coast market. At the same time, traditional retailers began introducing elements of the Price concept, including bulk goods and heavy discounting, providing additional competition.

Over the next decade, both Price Club and Costco Wholesale continued to innovate and grow, and in 1993, the two mega-retailers merged, officially making business partners of Price and Sinegal and making Costco the world's most successful warehouse club.

Sinegal served as its president and CEO until 2012 and was known for his smart and caring style of management rooted in the belief that employees who are treated well will, in turn, treat and serve customers well. For example, through Costco, he provided his employees—at every level of the company, even part-time employees who work an average of 23 hours per week—compensation and benefits that were much higher than retail industry norms.[10] He later said in an interview that there was a lot more to success than pleasing Wall Street analysts who criticized him for placing favorable treatment of employees and customers ahead of pleasing shareholders. Investors might want higher earnings, but Sinegal stated, "We want to build a company that will still be here 50 or 60 years from now."[11] A 2012 CNBC documentary stated that from 1985 until Sinegal's retirement, the stock's value had increased by five *thousand* percent.[12] When we discuss the customer value to be found in new business models, we'd be doing a disservice not to include how that model transcends to its employees and what role that may play in the success of the company.

Today, 100 million members shop 4,000 types of items (in contrast, the average supermarket sells 40,000 types of items and Walmart stocks about 125,000 types of products) at over 780 warehouses worldwide. Starting around 2005, the company slowly expanded its sales model to include the Costco Auto Program, Costco Optical, Costco Travel, and its own private label, Kirkland Signature. It's a business model that works, generating over $149 billion in annual sales, and it all started by having an exceptionally different business model.

SOCIETAL TRENDS

A fourth type of change that creates customer value is to take advantage of societal trends. The shifts in economic, environmental, technological, and ethical trends can and should impact your business strategy, and being aware of where people are—that is, knowing what people care about—can go a long way in securing customer value. Brands like Lululemon Athletica, GoPro, REI, Swatch, Nike, Fitbit, and Honda all cater to today's cultural climate—*I want to be healthier; I want to save the planet; I want to limit my screen time*—and are successful because of it.

After noticing more and more people sign up for yoga in the late 1990s, Chip Wilson bet everything on an athletic apparel company aimed toward young professional women. With the offering of a higher-end alternative to plain cotton leggings that would be comfortable, attractive, and fare well in a hot yoga studio, Lululemon spawned a new fashion trend and a new market (officially dubbed "athleisure") and forever changed what women—and more recently men—wear to work out.

Yes, Lululemon capitalized on the uptrend of sweat-inducing yoga, but it also capitalized on the societal fervor over sustainability and carbon footprint reduction by asserting that environmental health is the foundation of personal health. Through products aimed toward self-care, processes that abide by ethical standards, and an ambassador program that stretches across the globe, Lululemon played into the priorities and enthusiasm of its customers and were able to morph from just an apparel company to a lifestyle brand that's synonymous with feeling good about how you look, healthy living, and mindfulness. What started as a small pop-up store in Vancouver eventually became a multibillion-dollar company that has over 400 stores across 14 countries and a strong web presence, proving that aligning your business strategy with today's societal trends, like health and wellness, can pay off in a huge way.

Restaurants have been in the throes of shifting societal trends in recent years, mainly in regards to consumer eating habits and the redefinition of convenience. For decades, baby boomers focusing on career and family gravitated toward convenience foods that saved time: fast food and going out to restaurants. Today, convenience has extended to already prepared meals and quick delivery with a greater emphasis on healthy and natural foods. As one industry expert put it, consumers are going "in" to eat more. Almost 50 percent of meals purchased from a restaurant are eaten at home.[13]

Grocery stores are adjusting by adding more space for prepared and healthier foods and growing their e-commerce and online pickup businesses. In 2017, only 2 percent of all grocery sales were online, but a study by the Food Marketing Institute projects online grocery to capture 20 percent of total grocery retail by 2025.[14] Manufacturers are creating healthier foods that contain more natural ingredients and are reducing unhealthy ingredients, such as sugar and fat, in the foods they currently sell. Even appliances are adapting to the shifts—think of the 2019 rage around the Instant Pot as a perfect example.

Given these trends, the growth of online food delivery isn't surprising. Consumers are accustomed to shopping online for everything from clothes to gadgets to furniture, so why should dinner be any different? Delivery brings even more convenience. And in today's restaurant industry that's marred by fierce competition, tightening margins, and labor shortages, many restaurants are going the extra mile to meet customers where they are—and in this case, that means at home.

Still only a tiny percentage of restaurant orders, online food-delivery services like GrubHub, DoorDash, and Uber Eats earned over $22 billion in 2019 (and that was just in the United States—global food-delivery sales hit $107 billion[15]), and with an expected annual growth rate of 6.5 percent, it's projected to reach a market value of over $28 billion by 2023.[16] (For what it's worth, some analysts like Morgan Stanley project an even higher annual growth rate for online food delivery).[17] This is shocking information for anyone who remembers when meal delivery meant pizza and Chinese food.

For years, the most common form of delivery was the traditional model in which a consumer placed an order with a restaurant that offered delivery (like the aforementioned pizza parlor or Chinese restaurant) and then waited for the restaurant to bring the food to their door. However, as in so many other sectors, the rise of digital technology has reshaped the market, and a proliferation of delivery models and fleet types emerged in response: aggregators, new delivery apps, and full-stack delivery services; same-hour, same-day, and next-day delivery; and single-fleet, multi-fleet, crowdsourced fleets, and in-house fleets. Clearly, as the trend has progressed, so has the response.

For restaurants, online ordering and delivery has become an important way to create customer value; by allowing shifts in societal trends to directly influence their business strategy, they're managing to stay relevant and, in some cases, grow their business.

NEW MARKETS

The fifth type of change you can seek are new markets, new buyers, or new ways to think about a market. For example, not long ago, we didn't have bottled water. In fact, if someone came to me with that concept, I probably would've told them that the idea was idiotic. But it turned out to be a genius—not to mention lucrative—idea for an entirely new market. Interestingly, the backlash to the plastic waste of bottled water has created another new market for insulated, high-quality, usually stainless steel, reusable water bottles. Other examples like Bloomberg, eBay, Botox, Pampers, iPad, FedEx, Cirque du Soleil, and NCAA March Madness show us how moving into new territories and categories is a radical strategy that can create major potential for business growth and customer value.

I'm a big basketball fan. The NCAA tournament wasn't a big deal when I was growing up, but it has since turned into a huge business. The men's tournament originally started in 1939, but it wasn't until the 1980s that March Madness began capturing the imagination of sports fans across the country. NBC aired the tournament from 1969 to 1981, but in 1982, CBS gained the rights to the tournament, hired Billy Packer away from NBC, and began broadcasting the March Madness Selection Show.

The interesting thing is that CBS realized that the product—college basketball—was already terrific, it just needed to figure out how to let it market itself. By airing the Selection Show and hiring Billy Packer, the most high-profile college basketball analyst of the time (and perhaps of all time), and turning up the marketing, it put its product on display in a way that hadn't been done before. Because of these moves, the tournament has grown into a multibillion-dollar enterprise.

Today, the NCAA allows 68 teams to qualify for the "big dance" (versus eight teams when it first started). They're divided into four regions and organized into a single-elimination bracket, which predetermines, when a team wins a game, which team it will face next. The key word here? *Bracket.* Every year, a reported 40 million people fill out a collective 149 million brackets to predict the winners of each game in the tournament—in both formal contests and informal betting pools among friends or colleagues.[18]

In 2018, the estimated amount wagered on the tournament was $10 billion, which is an impressive number because average bets are only $30 dollars. March Madness profits for Las Vegas casinos hit $100 million, the four biggest sponsors—GM, Coca-Cola, Capital One, and AT&T—spent $255 million on advertising, the total TV ad revenue was $1.28 billion, and a record 80.7 million devices live-streamed the tournament, a popular method for checking out the games while at work.[19] Speaking of work, March Madness is driving employers mad as some estimate that the tournament costs them $1.3 billion per hour in lost productivity due to distracted employees.[20]

March Madness created a market all its own. You could argue that it's akin to the Super Bowl, but the NCAA tournament is 67 games long, and each game on the bracket averages 11.3 million viewers. Combined, that's an audience of 757.1 million (many consumers watch multiple games, so the total unique audience is just under 100 million).[21] The NFL Wild Card, divisional playoffs, conference championships, and Super Bowl itself average little more than 50 million viewers per game (again these numbers include people who watch multiple games). However, with only 11 games, that's only 550 million total, or a 207.1 million fewer eyeballs for networks and sponsors to advertise to.[22]

Marketers should tip their hats to CBS and the NCAA for their ingenious marketing. For one, they swiftly garnered mainstream awareness through their penchant for alliteration, creating brand identities for the entire tournament as well as the interim playoffs: March Madness, Sweet Sixteen, Elite Eight, and Final Four. Awareness then morphed into action through the introduction of the fan bracket, which didn't just spawn a new market but an entire industry.

NCAA March Madness has become a staple of popular culture, and despite the odds of predicting a perfect bracket being one in 9.2 quintillion[23] (you're much more likely to be killed by a shark, struck by lightning, or elected president of the United States), the bracket actually isn't about winning at all (though that would be nice—every year, Warren Buffett offers to pay $1 million a year for life to any employee of Berkshire Hathaway or its subsidiaries who accurately predicts the results of the first week of March Madness games). Instead, it gives people a tangible interest in a basketball game that they might not care about or normally follow. Like fantasy sports (a big reason for the growth in popularity of the National Football League), the bracket and tournament not only capture basketball fans but also the casual fan who wants to follow how he/she's doing with his bracket picks. That inclusivity alone is a priceless lesson in strategy, but perhaps what's most impressive is that the creation of March Madness combined all the aspects of the fifth type of change: new markets, new buyers, *and* new ways to think about a market.

Seeking change is all about cognizance; staying aware of the opportunities for change that are around us. From a biological perspective, humans are the most adaptive species on earth, and we got to where we are today because of our incredible ability to adapt, shift, and grow. It's part of the culture we live in, but it's also—quite literally—what we evolved to do. It's the same in business. Companies should be receptive and equipped to face and embrace change. Those who fail to do so will lose their competitive edge and ultimately fail to meet the ever-changing needs of their customers.

Here's a prime example (or a cautionary tale, depending on how you look at it): In 1976, the first consumer VHS player came out. That new technology created an opportunity—independent video stores. One year later, in 1977, that new business model led to something else: Blockbuster. The founder soon asked himself why should he have an independent video store when he could have a chain, franchise them, and build a huge business? The chain grew rapidly, and by the early 1990s, Blockbuster had thousands of stores in the United States, and its worth was estimated at $4.6 billion.

And then in the early 2000s, the DVD came along. Its technology created another opportunity: Netflix. Reed Hastings was tired of paying late fees, so he created a mail order DVD rental business. Customers could simply choose how many rental DVDs they wanted at any one time and mail them back whenever they were done with them. (No more late fees!) The iconic Netflix red envelope was well known and used by millions. Well over ten million people subscribed to the Netflix DVD service at one point, and surprisingly, well over two million still subscribe to the DVD-by-mail part of its business as of 2019. Netflix has shipped enough red envelopes to wrap the world in paper 48 times.[24]

Important to note here is that Hastings called the company Netflix, not DVDflix. He anticipated what was going to happen next: Broadband, which completely changed everything yet again. Broadband created new opportunities by making streaming possible and attracted new players: Amazon Prime, Hulu, Xfinity, HBO Go, Xbox Live, Showtime, and Chromecast are just a small handful of the media players that were either formed or impacted as a result. So from 1976 until now, there's been a complete transformation of the business multiple times, and that change—or, the people who took advantage of that change—were the people who were successful with their strategies and their businesses.

Who didn't take advantage of the change? Blockbuster. When they started losing customers to competitors, they stood firm in their outdated business model of physical stores, rental periods, and late fees, and began squeezing the most out of that existing structure with more expensive late fees and quicker rental times. They were focused on bringing in more money rather than innovating their products to earn the right to charge more; they were consumed with keeping their model alive rather than remembering the purpose behind it. If Blockbuster would have concentrated on providing a better movie-in-your-home experience, they just might still be around.

Instead, Blockbuster pissed off Reed Hastings by charging him a $40 late fee for an overdue rental of *Apollo 13*, and in his frustration, he got the idea for Netflix. What's more, he approached Blockbuster in 2005 with the option to buy Netflix for $50 million. Years later, Netflix co-founder Marc Randolph recalled that meeting. Blockbuster CEO John Antioco wore "loafers that probably cost more than my car" and used all the typical tricks from Business Meetings 101: lean in, make eye contact, nod slowly when the speaker turns in your direction, and frame questions in a way that makes it clear you're listening. But after Hastings named the $50 million number, Randolph saw Antioco's demeanor change and watched his mouth involuntarily turn up at the corner; he was struggling not to laugh. The meeting went downhill pretty quickly after that. Netflix was more or less laughed out of the room. Afterward, Randolph recalled saying it was clear that, "Blockbuster doesn't want us, so it's obvious what we have to do now. It looks like now we're going to have to kick their ass."[25] And they did.

Blockbuster didn't embrace inevitable change and lacked the vision to see where the industry was going, and because of this wound up filing for bankruptcy in 2010. At the time, the company was valued at around $24 million, while Netflix's worth was around $13 billion—and that was just barely after Netflix added to its DVD-by-mail subscription service with online streaming. Today, Netflix has award-winning original programming, is an official member of the Motion Picture Association of America (the first for a streaming digital media company), and has over 167 million subscribers.[26]

Even with Netflix's dramatic success, it continues to face challenges like increased competition, maintaining new subscriber growth, rising content costs, and losing key parts of its catalogue. But the company is still the original poster child for adaptability, and the facts behind its ascension remains the same: Netflix treated change as an opportunity. In fact, all the successful companies we've highlighted in this chapter did so. Whether it was through technology, innovation, new business models, societal trends, or new markets, every company took a strategic approach to change management and flourished because of it. The tactics they used in seeking change weren't revolutionary. Instead, they were intentional, informed, and timely. And when it comes to the Strategy = E × mc² formula, employing those tactics can be the tipping point in securing customer value.

Which type of change resonates the most with you and your endeavors? What deliberate action can you introduce into your business strategy? What kind of change can you seek that will distinguish you from your competitors and differentiate your customer value?

CHAPTER 4

Mine the Gaps

Do you remember the great first-mover movement of the early 2000s? The idea, which has been around for eons and gained an intense following during the dot-com mania, was that the initial ("first-moving") significant occupant in a given market gained an advantageous and perhaps insurmountable market position just by being first. (The key words here are *significant occupant* because a first-mover advantage doesn't necessarily mean the first company to launch has the advantage, but rather, the advantage goes to the first company to capture large market share.) The theory had legs. Some well-known first movers—Sony in personal stereos, Coca-Cola in soft drinks, Hoover in vacuum cleaners, Amazon in online book sales, eBay in online auctions—have enjoyed considerable success. But, not surprisingly, it doesn't always work that way.

DuMont led the way in selling TV sets when they were new devices, but the company lost out to latecomers like RCA and Motorola who themselves lost out to companies that lead television sales today like Samsung, LG, and Sony. Chux was the leading disposable diaper yet succumbed to Procter & Gamble's Pampers. Ampex had a commanding position in video recorders for two decades until Sony took over. Pfizer's Listerine PocketPaks breath strips were an immediate hit but got overshadowed by copycat products from Altoids and Ice Breakers. Sidecar was the pioneer of ride sharing, yet Uber and Lyft now dominate the market. Netscape was an early-to-market internet browser and a market leader until the rise of Microsoft's Internet Explorer, which then lost its leadership to Google Chrome. The iPhone wasn't the first smartphone; Facebook wasn't the first social network.

It turns out that often the competitors who come later are the big winners. In every business, there are gaps you can mine—pockets of untapped potential where you can pan for gold and wield your pickaxe to find opportunities to unearth. Gaps can be described as areas where there is no competition or areas where a competitor is doing a poor job. Gaps can also occur when there are changes in a business that create gaps. It's all about finding an "in" by identifying advantages and ramping up customer value, market potential, or execution; or finding often disguised opportunities and then throwing ingenuity and resources into solving those problems.

SEARCHING FOR GAPS

Circa 1998, there were plenty of search engines to choose from: America Online (AOL), Lycos, WebCrawler, Yahoo, HotBot, MSN, Ask Jeeves, and AltaVista just to name a few. Though, as you may or may not remember, none of them had very good search capabilities; they weren't that thorough or user-friendly, and they had a lot going on. They were littered with ads. Some wanted you to edit results, and others wanted you to drill down your results through the use of key words. Then along came Google to blow them all out of the water.

There are numerous reasons why Google was such a superior option, some of which are still relevant today. For one, Google ranked search results using a trademarked algorithm called PageRank, which assigned each web page a relevancy score, so the odds of it pulling up what you're looking for generally exceeded its competitors. Two, it featured a search bar and little else, making it simple to use and abundantly clear to the user that searching was the primary function of the site. (Bing, the distant second place alternative to Google, basically copied this feature when it launched in 2009). And three, Google understood better than any other company that, at the time, a search engine's sole purpose was to get rid of users as quickly as possible. Most of these advantages have been copied now, but at the time, Google was an anomaly.

Search engines weren't originally made to be destinations; they were specifically designed to act as a middleman between your question and the site with the answer. Whichever site got you to your destination quickest, no matter the complexity of your query, is the site you'd find most useful, right? No other search engine mastered that concept like Google. In the 1990s, most internet executives believed that for a web service to be profitable, it had to be, in essence, like a TV show—meaning it had to hold its users' attention long enough to deliver advertising. This ability to hold attention was known as "stickiness" and was the most desired web metric at the time. Just as TV viewers would endure commercials in order to watch great programming, so the executives reasoned, they'd endure advertisements in order to get their queries answered for free. And the longer users stayed on the page, the more advertising a search engine could sell.

Google refused to play that game, and in their early years, it was sometimes to their detriment. When they tried to sell their technology to Excite, one of the leading portal/search engines in the late 1990s, the deal was a non-starter. Excite's CEO thought if they were to host a search engine that instantly gave people the information they sought, users would leave the site immediately. Since ad revenue at Excite came from people staying on the site, using Google's technology would be counterproductive. When explaining his refusal to make a deal, the CEO told Google executives that he wanted Excite's search engine to only be 80 percent as good as the other search engines.[1] He was more concerned about generating revenue than search efficiency.

Google has proven to be the one search engine with staying power. Google figured out where competitors were missing the mark—relevance, reliability, and ease of use being the three biggest gaps—and then accommodated the need. By formulating a smarter algorithm and throwing the status quo of stickiness, clutter, and excessive advertising out the window, Google gained a massive edge and a massive audience. I may be being a bit harsh on the other search vendors, but if you calculate an SFS for Google versus its competitors circa 2003 or so, Google would get a 4 on execution and the other players a 2.

Internet Search *Circa 2003*

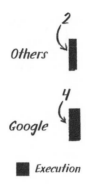

Others

Google

■ *Execution*

Market potential for both would be a 5.

Internet Search *Circa 2003*

Others

Google

■ *Execution*   ▨ *Market Potential*

And I would give Google a customer value score of 4 versus giving a 2 to the other search vendors.

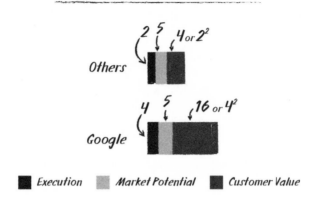

As you can see, Google's advantage really stands out.

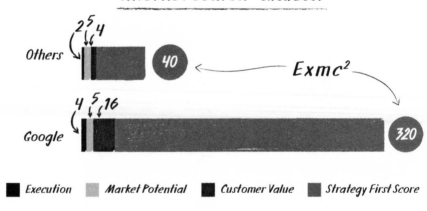

Ironically, the Excite CEO's desire to keep search users on his site may have been more prescient than the history books realized. Much has changed with search technology and usage, and some of what made Google search successful in the first place has now shifted. Google is no longer just helping users find something elsewhere; now it gives them the answers they need right on the Google search results page. It's faster for consumers to get the answers they want, and it's more profitable for Google. Ask for the weather in your hometown, and Google will give you the answer without you having to click on a link. Type in the movie you want to see, and show times come up immediately. In fact, a recent study concluded that more than 50 percent of Google searches end without a click to other content.[2] Welcome to the world of zero-click searches.

Google's approach has translated to its ever-increasing dominance of the search engine market; as of 2019, the company owns 88 percent of it.[3] This proves the power of prioritizing customer value while also understanding how to generate monstrous revenue and profit from the advertising business. Because searching the internet is context sensitive, it is an ideal advertising platform; if you're searching for a dishwasher, you are likely looking to buy one and thus manufacturers and sellers of dishwashers have a great platform to advertise with search products. But to gain the top spot in Google advertisements, advertisers have to outbid each other. Higher bids move up the list of results while low bids may not even be displayed.

Google has built an ad platform called Google Ads (previously called AdWords) to sell key words, display ads, product listings, and so on across its extensive ad network which includes not only Google Search but also its other properties, such as YouTube, Gmail, and Google Maps. Google Ads is responsible for most of Google's advertising revenue. Google has other key advertising products, such as AdSense, which allows Google to publish ads on partner websites—the Google Marketing Platform, a unified advertising and analytics platform for Google's marketing services and digital ads, and the Google Ads Manager, where Google helps websites sell their excess ad inventory. Put it all together, and Google is an advertising behemoth. Google's early gap mining has turned into a gargantuan gold mine. In 2019, Google's ad revenue was a whopping 134.8 billion US dollars.[4]

People think of Google as a search engine, and it is, but Google is also an advertising company. And to personalize ads and maximize the potential revenue from its advertising customers, Google collects tons of your personal information from the plethora of its products, such as Google search, Android phones, Google Home, and YouTube. Google will also eventually collect your personal data from Fitbit, its recent smartwatch company acquisition. The Department of Health and Human Services is even opening an inquiry about Project Nightingale, a Google partnership with Ascension, the second-largest healthcare system in the United States, that reportedly collects patient information about millions of Americans.[5] Sometimes Google even collects data about you from public sources. Google outlines the type of information it collects in its privacy policy, and consumers can request a copy of the personal information Google has tracked about them. Though Google also gives consumers the ability to limit what information is stored, I doubt many customers read the Google privacy policy or take advantage of that option.

In December 2017, one CNBC reporter noted that Google had collected his name, gender, and birthdate; his personal cell phone numbers; his recent Google searches; the YouTube videos he's watched; the websites he visited; the fact that he turned on his bedroom lights the night before he wrote his article; exactly where he'd been over the past several years; that he likes American football, games, jazz, and audio equipment; his favorite food and drink; where he works and lives; and more.[6] Combine Google's search market share with its ability to personalize advertising via the data it collects, and Google becomes a daunting company to compete against.

Why did Google attempt to compete with Facebook by introducing Google+? Because Facebook is also an advertising company, and Google sees Facebook as a competitor. Both companies now likely see Amazon's growing clout in online advertising as a threat to their advertising business as well, and Google and its advertising competitors have more than each other to worry about because governments and consumers are increasingly concerned about their dominant positions. In Google's case, Google's search success is so large and encompassing that it is constantly under scrutiny from regulators around the world worried about anti-trust and Google abusing its commanding market share. In fact, since 2017, the European Commission has ruled that Google violated anti-trust or anti-competitive laws three different times and has fined the company in total over $9 billion.[7]

THERE ARE GAPS TO MINE EVERYWHERE

Google certainly wasn't the first, or the last, to mine a gap—tons of companies have observed underperforming competitors and then capitalized on unrealized execution or customer-value opportunities. Netflix provided convenience through DVD rentals by mail with its iconic red envelope. LaCroix gave consumers a flavored, guilt-free soda alternative with no artificial sweeteners. Redfin allowed the general public to search for property listings online and offered salaried (versus commissioned) real estate agents. Whole Foods offered health-conscious consumers a central place to shop and dine on natural, organic, and high-quality food products. Bird e-scooters negated car usage, traffic, and congestion by providing people with readily accessible transportation. All of these brands and countless more had a distinct edge they used to mine some sort of untapped market gap and produce something that would be uniquely valuable for consumers.

But gaps aren't limited to tangible, appreciable products. Take Janice Bryant Howroyd and her employment agency, ActOne. When she moved to Los Angeles as a new college graduate in the late 1970s, she got a temp job as a secretary at *Billboard* magazine. While there, she noticed there were lots of other executives who needed good clerical help, and they needed it fast; it seemed they just didn't have the time to find the right people.

Hiring employees is one of the hardest things about running a business. When companies start to scale, hiring enough good people consumes employers' time because hiring requires patience, research, and well, luck. Even the best applicants sometimes fail after they start. Janice wanted to make the process of finding employment an easier one—for both the worker, whether temporary or permanent, and the employer— but more than that, she wanted to ensure the employee was a good fit for everyone involved. Was there a more surefire way to set people up for success? Those were the insights and questions Janice came across early in her career, and ultimately, it's what led her to do what she did next.

With all the money she had at the time, which was $1,500, Janice rented a small space in front of a rug shop in Beverly Hills and started an employment agency. She was a young African American woman starting out in an industry dominated by older white men, and with only a fax machine and a telephone, she set out to put humanity back in human resources. From the get-go, she was all about the prospective hire; she paid special attention to the strengths of each applicant before trying to find them an employer, and she prided herself on "acting as agents for them, if you will."[8] It was certainly a different approach than other companies within the industry had ever taken, and one that prioritized her personal business protocol and life mantra: "Never compromise who you are personally to become what you wish to be professionally."

She started by making full-time job placements for companies needing workers and then shifted to temporary placements. Slowly, she added new divisions to ActOne in order to fill various employer needs, like employee screening and payroll. Over the next three decades, Janice grew ActOne to be the largest privately held, woman-owned workforce management company in the United States. Today, it has 17,000 contracts in 19 countries, provides staffing across many, many industries—including niche ones like healthcare, STEM, and IT—and generates more than $1 billion in annual revenue.[9] ActOne mined a gap—not by offering a service that no one else did, but offering that service in a *way* that no one had before.

A similar paradigm is found in the world of insurance. Insurance is a formality, a hope-you-never-need-it safety net, and a huge business. In 2015, US carriers collected over $1.27 trillion in premiums, about 7 percent of gross domestic product (GDP).[10] In that same year, the property-casualty insurance industry spent $6.5 billion on advertising.[11] Are the astronomical marketing budgets worth it? You tell me. If I list the catchphrases, spokespeople, or mascots from a handful of insurance companies, would you be able to tell me which company goes with which advertising campaign? Here we go:

- Their spokesman is Green Bay Packers quarterback Aaron Rodgers.

- Each commercial ends with, "And be better protected from mayhem . . . like me."

- Their mascot is a white duck.

- Actor J. K. Simmons recounts outrageous insurance claims and says, "We know a thing or two because we've seen a thing or two."

- Over 100 of their commercials feature Flo, the fictional salesperson who always wears a white apron and red lipstick.

- Peyton Manning, retired NFL all-star quarterback, is their spokesperson and their tagline jingle is "They are on your side."

- Their mascot is an animated gecko who speaks with a Cockney accent.

Did you guess State Farm, Allstate, Aflac, Farmers, Progressive, Nationwide, and GEICO? And these represent only a small portion of the industry, because I didn't include anything from other huge players like, Liberty Mutual, The General, or MetLife. Insurance is clearly a highly publicized industry, but that wasn't always the case. Not until one company in particular mined a gap and changed the landscape of that market forever.

Until the 1990s, if you needed auto insurance, you picked up the phone and called your neighborhood agent or visited their storefront. But once the internet arrived, those business models became less apropos; they weren't the most efficient or instinctual way to go about securing insurance anymore. GEICO recognized and capitalized on the opportunity. And if you dig into their company history, it's not too surprising that they were the ones to do so.

GEICO was founded by Leo Goodwin Sr. and his wife Lillian in 1936 as auto insurance specifically for federal government employees and their families (hence the words behind the acronym: Government Employees Insurance Company). In 1974, they began to insure the general public, selling directly to consumers at a lower cost than their competitors. Analysts believed GEICO would never be able to compete with the larger insurance firms and their armies of sales agents because their distribution model defied conventional wisdom. But GEICO did compete. In fact, they became unlikely contenders that thrived in their niche and radically changed the game.

In the 1980s, GEICO pioneered the 24-hours a day, 365-days a year call center for claims and sales, which increased their level of automation and decreased their costs associated with conducting business. They became prudent with their underwriting, with loss adjustment and general expenses that typically amounted to just 25 percent of premiums—at times 10 to 15 percentage points lower than their competitors. GEICO expanded their offerings to include homeowners and life insurance, all while continuing their refusal to use middlemen agents. By the end of the decade, GEICO had turned into a major insurance enterprise that dominated the industry. And then in 1996, after many years as a publicly traded firm, they became a wholly owned subsidiary of Berkshire Hathaway.

It was a real full circle moment, and here's why: Toward the beginning of GEICO's eight-decade history, in 1951, a Columbia University business student named Warren Buffett became interested in the company after he found out his favorite professor and burgeoning mentor, Benjamin Graham, was its chairman. After immersing himself in the ins and outs of what he called "[to me] an unknown company in an unknown industry," Buffett finished at Columbia, returned to his hometown of Omaha to sell securities, and focused almost exclusively on GEICO.

He wrote a short report about the company for "The Security I Like Best" column in *The Commercial and Financial Chronicle*, a leading financial publication of the time, and then proceeded to buy stock for his own account, investing more than half of his $20,000 net worth.[12] It was one of the first major investments the future billionaire would make and one of the first examples of his uncanny ability to spot undervalued stocks. Buffett ended up selling his GEICO stock in order to invest in Western Insurance Specialties—a decision he'd later regret: "The GEICO stock I sold grew in value to about $1.3 million, which taught me a lesson about the inadvisability of selling a stake in an identifiably-wonderful company."

Buffett became a millionaire by 1962 and formed an investment group that took control of Berkshire Hathaway—the textile manufacturing company turned multinational conglomerate holding company—by 1965. In the mid-1970s, Buffett returned to his "first business love" by opening up Berkshire's thick wallet to purchase $45.7 million worth of GEICO shares, which translated to a 15 percent stake in the company. Twenty years later, after his initial investment grew to be worth more than $2 billion, and he owned 50 percent of the company, Buffett announced his intention to acquire the remaining shares in GEICO, which he did for $2.3 billion. He later attributed much of Berkshire Hathaway's profit increases during the following two years to the acquisition.

MINE THE MARKETING GAPS

You may think these examples of GEICO's gap mining are impressive—their revolutionary direct-to-consumer business model and establishment of the call center—but I actually haven't gotten to their most significant contribution on the minefield yet. There was a considerable, and more recent, opportunity GEICO seized that catapulted their brand, exponentially increased the value they provided to customers, and allowed them to net a significant portion of the market share of the US insurance market: the prioritization of marketing. While both GEICO and their competitors had long used television, radio, and direct mail to promote their products and services, it wasn't until GEICO invested wildly in their advertising that they solidified themselves as an industry standard.

Wherever you went, whatever medium you consumed, there were GEICO ads. And it wasn't just volume that was key; it was cleverness. Their ad campaigns were light-hearted, funny, and memorable. Instead of following the predominant formula that focused on the catastrophic events that consumers needed insurance for—images of car accidents, fires, floods, or burglaries with a voice-over that offered reassurance about how all would be well for those who chose the right coverage—GEICO believed that its target audience thought insurance was boring, the products were all similar, and that insurance was a burden. In that case, why not lighten the burden? Why not infuse some satire and set themselves apart from competitors?

That decision was the game changer. Well, specifically, the gecko was the game changer. You know him well. The little green reptile was the brainchild of the Martin Agency, a Virginia-based advertising agency that's worked with GEICO since 1994 and has served several purposes: The first was reinforcing GEICO's name, the second was helping the public figure out how to pronounce it, and the third was addressing an unexpected need.

In May 2000, the Screen Actors Guild (SAG) and the American Federation of Television and Radio Artists (AFTRA) went on strike against the advertising industry over commercial work compensation. Since rumblings of a strike had been going on for some time, entire industries had been preparing and weighing their options for its likelihood, which would prevent 135,000 actors from working. Some companies dug up previously used commercials, and others scraped together members of their production staff to fill in for the actors. GEICO decided to go a different route: computer-generated imagery (CGI).

Although CGI wasn't new, per se, it was primarily used in film, not commercials. Suffice it to say, an insurance company that used it for a humorous television ad starring an animated reptile was a bold and innovative move. Do you remember the original commercial? The gecko climbed onto a podium with a microphone and with his Cockney accent said, "This is my final plea: I am a gecko, not to be confused with GEICO, which could save you hundreds on car insurance. So, stop calling me!" before licking his eye. It hit the airwaves, and the rest, as they say, is advertising history.

Since then, GEICO has rolled out many well-known ad campaigns that have introduced numerous characters and themes into pop culture. While the gecko remains their main mascot, there's also the recurring

GEICO Cavemen, Maxwell the Pig, the googly-eyed stack of cash (aptly named Kash), and the Hump Day Camel. Then there's the cyclic marketing like the Rhetorical Questions campaign that always starts with, "Could switching to GEICO really save you 15 percent or more on car insurance?" and is followed up with a line like, "Does it take two to tango?"; the Good News campaign where one character breaks bad news to another and ends with, "But I've got good news! I just saved a bunch of money on my car insurance by switching to GEICO." And this is only a partial list of GEICO's well-known campaigns.

Aside from GEICO's impressive levels of production and creativity, the most notable thing about their marketing is that they run different ad campaigns concurrently, each with the company's own unique tone, style, flavor, and message. At one time, they'll broadcast up to six different campaigns that appeal to a broad range of target audience segments.

Ask any brand builder in the world, and they'll tell you that using a seemingly disjointed and eclectic lineup of ads is the wrong way to create a cohesive, focused brand image. They'll tell you that consistency is the key to shaping people's perceptions and getting your messages to stick. GEICO doesn't just ignore these widely accepted branding "rules," they do everything possible to break them. They take saturation to an entirely new level, but they do it in a way that keeps their content fresh and original. They originated that unorthodox marketing strategy, and in doing so, filled a void that no one else even knew was there.

You may argue that the downside of all this marketing is the exorbitant cost associated with generating so much original content and using up so much airtime. You're not wrong. In an industry that spends close to $7 billion a year in advertising, GEICO is the only brand that surpasses the $1 billion mark, by far the largest share. But at an annual Berkshire

Hathaway meeting, Buffett said, perhaps half-jokingly, that he would double the advertising expenditure to $2 billion if he could.[13]

While they haven't gone there yet, their enormous marketing budget is an important facet of their business strategy and a luxury other competitors don't have, because it's offset by not paying agents commissions or overhead for a broad brick-and-mortar presence. Even then, their advertising costs could still seem excessive, but a 2016 study of over 1,000 insurance companies found that those who spend at least 15 percent of their revenue on marketing are more likely to see "significant revenue growth" of at least 20 percent year over year. Brands that spend less than 5 percent, on the other hand, are three times as likely to see zero growth.[14]

In addition to mining the marketing and brand-building gap, GEICO also foresaw the importance of having an online presence. In the early 2000s, as the internet was gradually shifting from communications technology (mailing lists, emails, online forums, and bulletin boards) into a key part of global society's infrastructure (commerce, services, applications, blogs, social media, news, and entertainment/ streaming), GEICO saw the opportunity for a low-involvement product: buying insurance online. Because GEICO was already the pioneer of customer independence through their lack of agents, a website where you could conveniently get a quote and purchase coverage with the click of a button was a natural next step. At the time, there was only one other insurance company that offered such a service to their customers, though they didn't have near the brand recognition that GEICO had. GEICO bet on their familiarity and wide reach to drive traffic to a website, and by 2004, you couldn't miss the Cavemen ads touting that geico.com was "so easy even a caveman could do it."

Soon, rivals in their category took note and launched interactive and user-friendly websites of their own, along with marketing efforts that attempted to reach the same level of brand-building, memorability, frequency, and humor that GEICO's bar had set. (Today, you'd be hard-pressed to find an insurance commercial that doesn't go for the laugh.) But once a miner, always a miner. GEICO soon combined their marketing prowess with their digital presence, getting creative with how to get in front of more people and how to stand out while doing it.

You know the pre-roll ads that air before most videos on YouTube—the ones you can't skip until they've run for five seconds? GEICO decided to have some fun and see if they could get the viewer to not want to skip the ad at all. The premise of the ads was always the same: Within the first five seconds, a situation involving two or more actors warrants the commercial announcer to explain how GEICO could save them 15 percent or more on car insurance, followed by a very quick, "You can't skip this GEICO ad because it's already over." Set to intentionally cheesy music and with the GEICO logo unabashedly huge in the middle of the screen, they've already succeeded by getting their message out within the five-second window.

Then, if the viewer hangs in there beyond the time where they can skip the ad, that's when the good stuff kicks in. The live actors attempted to mimic a freeze-frame, often in awkward situations, and the events turn disastrous. In one such ad, two friends high-five over their savings at a barbeque, but as they stop moving, suspended in midair, the stunt wires become visible and one of the actors drops his tongs, starts coughing from the grill's flames, and his foot catches fire. In another, a family is freeze-framed around the dinner table when their dog comes in and eats the spaghetti from the father's plate.

In the world of unskippable pre-roll ads that are usually devoid of anything worth watching, GEICO got creative and gave viewers a pay-off. The ads, which ranged from 30 seconds to over a minute in their entirety, clocked more than 14 million views.[15] They were named *Ad Age*'s 2016 Campaign of the Year and earned the Film Grand Prix at the Cannes Lions International Festival of Creativity. Seeing the success of this surprising niche, GEICO doubled down and, by 2018, was the top advertiser on YouTube, supplying 6 percent of its revenue.[16]

GEICO knows it takes money to make money. Is this massive ad working for them? Without a doubt. Since 1998, GEICO has seen an increase in underwriting profit in all but one year, which is especially commendable because most property and casualty insurers are happy to break even on their underwriting and make their profits on investments. Their number of policyholders has risen from 5 million in 2002 to 8 million in 2007 to 17 million in 2019.[17]

GEICO secured its place as an insurance powerhouse by finding and mining major gaps in the insurance business with its massive advertising campaigns that built its brand and garnered awareness and revenue. They took advantage of the internet and the opportunities it provides for consumers to easily purchase auto insurance online, had a laser focus on brand management and strategic target markets, and were backed by one of the most dependable leaders in business, Warren Buffett. They became a unique player in an established market and found success through standing out—not only by embracing how they were different but also by relying on those differences to be the very things that give them value. What would happen if every business saw its differences that way?

The same type of tactics have been deployed by all the examples I've covered, from Google to companies like Netflix, Redfin, Whole Foods, and ActOne. They show that gaps are everywhere—pockets of opportunity, large and small, that current businesses aren't exploiting. Those unfulfilled needs can be met in big and little, drastic and subtle ways, and it all starts with awareness. That is, seeing the market landscape both for what it is and what it could be and then getting strategic about how to get from point A to point B. How can you mine that gap to outflank your competitors?

CHAPTER 5

Adapt to the Tides

How many pictures and videos do you take on your phone per week? And how many stay on there, not to be looked at again, until you're out of storage and forced to scroll back through and delete? Despite having the smartest phones with the most cutting-edge technology at our fingertips (quite literally), to have our multimedia living out their days inside our phones is a relatively common complaint. But with tons of services like Instagram, Google Photos, Flickr, Facebook, and cheap or free messaging, it's far less of a problem than it used to be. In the early 2000s, having photos and videos stuck forever in phone limbo land was the probable outcome for those who had camera phones.

One of the first publicly available phones with a built-in camera was the Nokia 7650, which boasted "a large 176 x 208 pixel colour display," according to a media release at the time.[1] (For the sake of comparison, the screen on the today's iPhone 11 Pro Max has a resolution of 2688 x 1242 pixels.) There was no zoom, no flash, no editing capabilities, and after snapping your photo, not many choices for where the photo could go. You could either use it as the phone's background picture, assign it to an entry in your contact list, play the pre-installed game Mix Pix that sliced your photos into tiny squares and mixed them up so you could piece them back together for fun, or send it to someone via Bluetooth or multimedia messaging service (MMS) for a hefty charge per message. Suffice it to say that most people never got their camera phone pictures off their phones.

Around that time, ex-Microsoft engineer Mike Toutonghi had an audacious vision to mine that gap; he wanted to create a way for everyone to easily share content from their phone to any device. His startup, Vizrea, officially launched in August 2003 as a photo-sharing service that centered around Nokia smartphones and worked like magic: You could sync your camera phone photo collections with your PC, send your pictures to a website for your friends to view, or send photos directly to your friends on their phones. All you needed was a data plan and the free Vizrea software, as did your friends if they wanted to swap pictures with you. In many ways, Vizrea was Instagram before Instagram.

But the "before" was part of the problem. As they say in venture capital circles, being early is the same as being wrong.[2] At that time, Nokia was well known for its flip phones; its poorly designed smartphones weren't very popular, especially in the United States. In addition, data plans were expensive and not nearly as ubiquitous as they are in much of the world today. Plus, data speeds were slow. Using the internet on a phone was like using an old dial-up modem on a computer, so pictures didn't send quickly. Combine all of those issues and Vizrea's super cool technology wasn't the revolutionary product that it could have or should have been.

Meanwhile, Apple's timing with the iPhone was excellent. It came out in 2007 right as data plan costs were getting more affordable and data speeds were getting faster with 3G (it featured quad-band GSM cellular connectivity with general packet radio service [GPRS], and EDGE for data transfer). The world was ready for it—in fact, six out of ten Americans surveyed at the time said they knew the iPhone was coming before its release[3]—and within 74 days, one million were sold.

As author and marketing guru Al Ries has said, "Strategy and timing are the Himalayas . . . everything else is the Catskills."

If you weren't one of the first million to purchase an iPhone, or one of the billion since, you're at least aware of the iPhone and its capabilities. I'm willing to bet the same can't be said of your familiarity with Vizrea. As I've discussed, a successful strategy can only be judged relative to its competition. Sometimes what separates competitors is how they adapt to the tides—that is, how a company understands what's going on in the external world and decides how those tides will impact their strategy. Vizrea was swimming against too many tides and made too many bad bets. Having the software only work on Nokia smartphones severely restricted market potential and customer interest, and the expense and slow speed of data plans restricted market potential and customer interest even further. They couldn't get any traction. If you think about it in terms of the Strategy = E × mc^2 formula, they didn't have enough customer value (not to mention they had poor execution since they chose to start with Nokia, a device that wasn't capable of making their technology relevant).

Just like a sailboat has to adapt to the tides (and the sun and the winds and more) to reach its destination or win a race, a company's stability and profitability are dependent on its ability to identify and respond to changes in the external environment, and while those external factors are uncontrollable, they don't have to be unforeseeable. In strategy parlance, various acronyms are used to summarize the various external factors that can affect a business. The one I use, not surprisingly, is TIDES:

- **T**echnology
- **I**nstitutional
- **D**emographics
- **E**conomic and environmental
- **S**ocial

In order to manage threats before they become significant problems, it's imperative to know the ins and outs of each factor and then use that knowledge to align your strategic plan to meet the changing demands in the marketplace.

TECHNOLOGY

TIDES starts with technology. We've covered the subject pretty extensively in regards to how it's been used to seek change and mine gaps, but how it differs here is this: Technology, more than any other external factor, is what evolves a market or industry—it catapults it forward. Technological advances have had dramatic strategic impacts and have fundamentally changed how business around the world is performed;

they're often at the root of a company's success or the reason behind its demise.

For almost a hundred years, Kodak was at the forefront of photography, with dozens of innovations and inventions—their roll film in 1885 became the basis for motion picture film; the Kodak camera in 1888 essentially marked the advent of amateur photography; the Brownie camera in 1900 introduced the snapshot to the masses; Kodachrome in 1935 was the first color film that used a subtractive color method, becoming the standard for movie-makers; the Super Kodak Six-20 in 1938 was the first camera to feature automatic exposure; the Instamatic camera in 1963 was the first compact camera on the market. In 1976, Kodak had an 85 percent market share of cameras and a 90 percent market share of film.[4] In 1981, their sales topped $10 billion. You get the picture (pun intended). But then, in 2012, they filed for bankruptcy.

What happened?

Digital cameras happened. And digital cameras were integrated into smartphones. And social media happened. And digital cameras, film, and photo printing became sideshows.

And Kodak was late to the party on all of the above.

What's ironic is that Kodak was all too familiar with digital cameras; they invented them. In 1975, an electrical engineer at Kodak named Steven Sasson invented a toaster-sized contraption that could save images using electronic circuits. The images were transferred onto a tape cassette and were viewable by attaching the camera to a TV screen, a process that took 23 seconds. It was an astonishing achievement, yet Sasson and his colleagues were met with blank faces when they unveiled the device to Kodak bosses. Mr. Sasson said, "But it was filmless photography, so management's reaction was, 'that's cute—but don't tell anyone about it.'" This was well before the digital age, and they didn't recognize the potential of what they were sitting on. A line from the technical report written at the time sums it up best: "The camera described in this report represents a first attempt demonstrating a photographic system which may, with improvements in technology, substantially impact the way pictures will be taken in the future."[5]

Thirteen years later, in 1988, when competitor Nikon released the first commercial DSLR camera, Kodak still wasn't focused on digital; they didn't want to diminish their film business, the company's golden egg. They ignored the axiom, "Better to cannibalize your own business than have someone else do so." Instead they wanted to diversify to new industries. That same year, 1988, Kodak acquired Sterling Drug, best known for Lysol cleaning products, Bayer aspirin, and Phillips' Milk of Magnesia, for $5.1 billion. Kodak hoped to use its expertise in chemical engineering to create profitable products, but it didn't work out as planned. Lacking pharmaceuticals expertise, Kodak dismantled the Sterling operations and sold off the remainder of their pharmaceutical business for less than $3 billion six years later.[6]

Though they went on to pour billions into developing technology for taking pictures using mobile phones and other digital devices and started selling digital cameras, Kodak continued to focus on analog cameras. They were losing money on digital cameras. According to a Harvard case study, Kodak lost $60 for every digital camera it sold by 2001.[7]

Kodak acquired Ofoto, an online digital photo developing service, in 2001 and turned it into Kodak Gallery. It featured online photo storage, sharing, personalized photo gifts, and photo viewing on mobile phones but was primarily centered around the business Kodak knew and was built on—getting users to print digital pictures. In fact, while uploading photos onto the site was free, those pictures were only stored for 90 days and then deleted unless users purchased prints or photo gifts. Kodak Gallery did okay for a while—in fact, at its peak in 2008, it reportedly served over 60 million users and hosted billions of images.[8] Kodak also briefly turned things around in its digital camera business in 2003, when the company released the EasyShare LS633 Digital Camera and Kodak EasyShare Printer, which focused on home photo printing. In 2005, Kodak was the largest digital camera seller in the United States (they were never strong outside of the United States).

But both the online photo sharing and the digital camera business improvements were short-lived. By 2007, Kodak had fallen to fourth place in US digital camera market share, and by 2010 Kodak was seventh.[9] But the digital camera business was doomed anyway. The biggest problem with Kodak's digital camera business, its home photo printer business, and the online storage and photo printing business is that they were all bad bets that ran into the rising tides of smartphones and subsequent rise of social media, which were making digital cameras and photo printing almost irrelevant and dramatically changing digital photo sharing. The relevance of digital cameras declined dramatically as smartphones got better and better at photography. Worldwide digital camera shipments have dropped 84 percent between their record sales year of 2010 and 2018.[10] Home photo printers and photo-sharing sites that focused on printing photos and photo gifts became niche markets as technology around social networking evolved. Consequently, Ofoto and the home photo printer business declined, and Kodak's digital cameras struggled even more in an already shrinking market.

It is worth getting into a little more depth on what happened with digital photo sharing. Originally, there were photo-sharing sites for storage like Zooomr, image organizer and editing sites like Picasa, photo printing and gift sites like Kodak Gallery, and more complete image hosting and sharing sites like Flickr. But social media changed all that as folks started posting and sharing their photos (and getting comments and likes) on Myspace and then Facebook, when it took over. Pinterest, Instagram, and Snapchat were soon to follow. That combination of mobile and social led to people sharing moments with photos and video way more often and in a totally different way than they used to with the early digital photo sites.

Today, there are still lots of sites that share and store photos as well as sell photo gifts, prints, books, and cards because there is still a need; these sites are better integrated with social media now, have good sharing features, and some are closely connected. They adapted to the tides when Kodak Gallery did not. Flickr is still a player, and this may be because of efforts to stay up to date on technology, such as adding video hosting to its repertoire. Google Photos is also a successful photo storage and sharing service. It gives users free, unlimited storage for photos up to 16 megapixels and videos up to 1080p resolution. The service automatically analyzes photos, identifying various visual features and subjects, helping users search for people, places, or things in their photos. Google Photos also backs up your mobile (and other) photos automatically, as do Apple iCloud, Microsoft OneDrive, Amazon Drive, and others. Imgur markets itself as a "community-powered entertainment destination" that lets you host images, videos, and GIFs. Sites like SmugMug (owner of Flickr) focus on more serious photographers and their needs. All these sites and more are to various degrees important to the photo business, though not at the center of the digital social sharing universe like Facebook, Instagram, Snapchat, and Pinterest.

It's not that Kodak should have come out with the digital camera in

1975 after Sasson initially invented it—for if they had, they would have surely met the same fate as Vizrea with their bad timing, unprepared customer base, and nonexistent market. But certainly, Kodak did not profit enough from its own innovation. That happened in other areas as well. In the 1970s, Kodak created the first viable OLED (organic light-emitting diode) display technology. In 2018, OLED was used in over 500 million mobile phones, digital cameras, VR headsets, tablets, laptops, and TVs. But Kodak missed the heyday of OLED by selling the business and its almost 2,000 OLED patents to LG in 2009 without having taken advantage of being a pioneer of the technology.[11]

Ultimately, Kodak could never get in front of the changing business tides. They'd adapted late to one trend, and just as they got some headwinds, the business changed yet again, and they fell behind. They didn't update their strategy as technology, social habits, and maybe even some demographic factors transformed the photo business right in front of them many times over. When the industry shifted from traditional film to digital photography, Kodak was late to the party. As the digital camera business was rapidly shrinking because of smartphones, Kodak got stuck flat-footed. When collecting and printing photos went the way of broad digital and social sharing, Kodak failed to realize that online photo sharing *was* the new business, not just a way to expand the printing business. "In law, we call it, a bird that likes to fly backward. Because it's more comfortable looking where it's been than where it's going," said Dan Alef, the author of a biography on George Eastman, the founder of Kodak.[12]

Contrast this with Kodak's longtime competitor, Fujifilm. Fujifilm faced the same sharp decline in its film products business, which in 2000 was 60 percent of its revenue and two-thirds of its profit. However, Fujifilm reinvented itself as a company to stay viable. The company did a technology audit and found new markets it could penetrate; it also made some acquisitions. For example, Fuji leads the market for protective LCD polarizer films used for TV, computer, and smartphones screens and is involved in healthcare via digital diagnostic imaging, digital printing, and digital publishing equipment. They are also the leader in the recording media market (like data backup tape cartridges) and make a number of industrial products.[13] Fujifilm's financial results illustrate how much Fujifilm has changed as a business. Today, the Imaging division is only 16 percent of revenue and 24 percent of the company's operating income.[14]

Kodak didn't successfully adapt to the tides where Fujifilm did—by shifting to many new businesses. But often, businesses that successfully adapt to the tides stay on course with their core business and use the change in tides to accelerate growth. TurboTax is a good example. TurboTax has used technology as an advantageous opportunity and, in doing so, forever altered an industry.

There used to be few standard options when it came to filing your tax returns: Use an independent CPA, go through a company like H&R Block or Jackson Hewitt, or try to navigate through all the forms and craziness by yourself and hope you did it right. But then Intuit's Turbo-Tax released a software program and became the bane of all professional tax preparers' existence (or they jumped on the bandwagon and used it themselves!). Initially developed in the mid-1980s, but not really gaining notable traction until the rise of the internet in the late 1990s, TurboTax offered taxpayers the luxury of do-it-yourself tax preparation through a user-friendly and efficient step-by-step process. It handled both state and federal income tax returns in one fell swoop, turned "e-file" into a common lexicon, and was free to use for some people who made less than $65,000 a year.

They mined a gap and then proceeded to dominate the market. Year over year, more and more people flocked to the digital tax-prep tool, and by 2018, TurboTax had nearly 35 million customers and a market share of 65 percent.[15] But they didn't stop there. They expanded their offerings to include a deluxe version that maximized tax deductions and credits, a premier version for those with investments and rental property, and a self-employed version that handled industry-specific deductions for people with personal and business income and expenses.[16]

Then, placing priority on their customers' use of smartphones, they launched a mobile app where you could snap a photo of your W-2, answer some questions, and e-file securely from your phone or tablet. They also added supplemental apps that did things like quickly estimate your tax refund, check your e-file status and tax refund timing, and track donations year-round.

Next, they addressed the need of filers who sought the confidence of having a tax pro by their side. They debuted TurboTax Live in 2018, which gave users virtual access to financial experts—all of them either CPAs, enrolled agents, or tax attorneys—who could give them personalized tax advice or review a return line by line via phone or one-way video.

When technology kept upping the ante, they doubled down. TurboTax repeatedly increased their investments in key technological areas like artificial intelligence, machine learning capabilities, migrating to Amazon Web Services and streamlining software development. They're a prime example of a company that has adapted to the tides instead of feeling threatened by the swell.

INSTITUTIONAL

The next external factor in TIDES is institutional impact, which encompasses the implications that both legal and political policies have on business strategies. For instance, current legal allowances like health and safety requirements, labor laws, and consumer protection laws affect how organizations operate. As do national, state, and local governments that influence certain industries through governmental regulations, political change, and trade and tax policy. Something as common as a shift in national leadership could have a significant effect on a business, as could legislation at the federal and state level, which might legally require a company to make changes to its operations, therefore becoming a critical success factor.

A great example of institutional impact is the US Postal Service (USPS) and how its regulations have led to the emergence of delivery businesses like FedEx and UPS to mine their gaps. The USPS is an independent agency of the executive branch of the US federal government (not to be confused with a government-owned corporation, like Amtrak) and has been around since 1775, when Benjamin Franklin was appointed as the first postmaster general. Over the past 240-plus years, there's been an enormous increase in the restrictions surrounding what it can and cannot do as an establishment.

We'll start with what they *can* do. Per the Private Express Statutes (PES)—a group of federal, civil, and criminal laws that place various restrictions on the carriage and delivery of letter mail—the USPS has a monopoly over the delivery of first-class residential mail. Further, the USPS is the only one granted access to customer mailboxes. Mail carriers work regular business hours six days a week. Mail sorters, on the other hand, work evening and night shifts, and all USPS locations get to observe national holidays.

The list of what they *can't* do, however, is much longer and the basis for which gap-mining for-profit express mail companies were built:

- The USPS has strict guidelines in terms of the size and weight of the packages it can send and deliver, as well as firm declarations about restricted (or outright banned) items that can't enter the mail stream.

- The USPS can only charge what Congress allows—this pertains to postage, priority mail fees, and packaging options—and increases require approval. There is also congressional pressure and oversight on where the USPS maintains postal offices, which is dependent on if Congress feels there is sufficient customer demand at specific locations (which, between you and I, is probably more about politics than customer demand).

- Any grievances of the USPS—be it geographic scope, range of products, access to services and facilities, delivery frequency, or affordable and uniform pricing—is not only out of its control, but cannot even be aired since it's prohibited from lobbying Congress.

In addition to oversight from Congress, the USPS is protected by more than 200 federal laws, and its policies and procedures are mandated by countless legislative acts and governing parties. That amounts to a lot of red tape, so it's no wonder that private parcel delivery services like FedEx and UPS aggressively leverage their differences and advantages.

FedEx was founded by its current chief executive, Fred Smith, in 1971. While a student at Yale in the mid-1960s, Smith submitted a term paper that laid out the logistical challenges facing pioneering firms in the information technology industry. He proposed a new concept where one logistics company would be responsible for a piece of cargo from local pickup to ultimate delivery, while operating its own aircraft, depots, posting stations, and ubiquitous delivery vans. Upon graduating, he began Federal Express based on that idea with a $4 million inheritance from his father and $91 million of venture capital.

The deregulation of the airline industry in 1977 helped Smith's cause because it meant the young company was able to purchase large jet aircraft to increase the number of packages that could be transported per day. FedEx bought seven Boeing 727 aircraft, followed by the purchase of Boeing 737 aircraft, and soon had 31,000 regular customers, including IBM and the US Air Force, which used them to ship spare parts. Further direct competition with USPS occurred when FedEx introduced the document-sized overnight letter for a flat fee. FedEx even made headlines promoting their new overnight delivery with an iconic, award-winning 1981 TV campaign where actor John "Motormouth" Moschitta Jr., speaking at a blistering 580 words or so a minute, pitched Federal Express overnight delivery as the panacea to deal with the fast-paced business world with the tagline, "When it absolutely, positively has to be there overnight."[17] When companies started to increase their use of overnight services, moving away from the USPS, it made FedEx the company with the largest sales of any US airfreight company.[18]

After several international acquisitions, worldwide service began. By 1989, FedEx was the world's largest full-service, all-cargo airline, with routes to 21 countries, and by 1994, that included sole aviation rights to the world's most populous nation, China. Today, that global reach expands to more than 220 countries and territories.[19]

UPS has been around far longer than FedEx, since the early 1900s, and it began as a messenger service that ran errands, delivered packages, and carried notes, baggage, and trays of food from restaurants. Messengers made most deliveries on foot and used bicycles for longer trips. By 1913, the young company was focused on package delivery for retail stores, and for about two years, their largest client was the USPS, for which they delivered all special-delivery mail entering Seattle—pretty ironic considering they would soon be direct competitors. Around 1922, UPS began to mine the gaps of USPS through offering automatic daily collection calls, acceptance of checks made out to the shipper in payment of CODs (collect on delivery), additional delivery attempts, automatic return of undeliverables, and streamlined documentation with weekly billing.[20]

Over the next five decades, UPS fought the US Interstate Commerce Commission to obtain authorization to ship freely in all 48 contiguous states, which was finally granted in 1975. Soon after, much like FedEx, they assembled their own jet cargo fleet and pursued the international shipping market. By 1989, UPS had a presence in six European countries, the Middle East, and Africa, and today they operate in more than 185 countries and territories.[21]

Both FedEx and UPS continue to capitalize on opportunities courtesy of the institutional limitations of the USPS: They deliver packages of virtually any size, have a far shorter list of prohibited items, offer overnight and early morning delivery options, provide customer-friendly pickup options, use superior tracking that offers the highest possible degree of precision, and work seven days a week, 365 days a year. It's worth noting too that the institutional limits and bureaucracy of USPS also make them less responsive to customer needs and changes. They could have potentially implemented some of these services—like I bet they could have done overnight delivery before FedEx—but they likely did not see the customer need.

I don't mean to downplay the impressive structure and hard work of the USPS; it's a well-oiled machine and a linchpin in a large and expansive industry. In 2018, 47 percent of the US mail volume—so, 146.4 billion units—was handled by the US Postal Service. Carriers delivered to 42,000 zip codes, accounted for 37 million address changes, and manned 31,324 post offices. It made $70.6 billion in operating revenue and had 497,157 career employees who got paid a collective $1.9 billion in salaries and benefits every two weeks. If it were a private sector company, it would rank 40th in the 2018 Fortune 500.[22]

But the USPS business is also decreasing. The volume of mail the USPS handles is down 30 percent since 2006. The rise of the internet has led to a material decrease in the use of first-class mail and marketing mail, two key parts of the USPS business.[23] The growth of package mail, where the USPS has substantial competition, has not compensated. USPS too has to learn to adapt to the tides.

That said, the upsides for USPS are in proportion to the constraints. Though there are benefits and clout from being intricately sewn into our economic fabric, those who are at the mercy of the government—meaning they're government-owned corporations or independent agencies of a particular branch of the government—will always be held to different standards. But that's not to say that governmental, political, or legal changes don't affect every American business in some way.

When it comes to you and your business strategies, what laws and regulations are governments or courts imposing that could help or hinder your success? How will changes in areas like labor, anti-trust, the environment, taxes, trade, and tariffs affect your business goals and outcomes? What waves will those factors create, and will they be big enough to threaten your buoyancy or create opportunities?

Businesses react to the world around them, as we've seen so far by looking at technological and institutional factors, and the same is true of the next one: demographics.

DEMOGRAPHICS

At its most basic, demography is the study of human populations. It takes into account statistical information like births, migration, aging, and death, thus allowing us to understand the size, structure, and distribution of the human population. It also considers the characteristics of a population, such as gender, race, age, education level, religion, occupation, income level, and marital status.

Being cognizant of and responsive to demographic trends—whether it's population shifts or lifestyle changes that are widely adopted by customers—will only strengthen a company's strategy. Think of it this way: Products are sold based on the strength of customer need. Knowing customers' needs starts with knowing where they are in life, literally and figuratively, and meeting them there.

In 1986, a guy named Antonio Swad moved to Dallas from Ohio to open a traditional pizzeria. Once there, he realized the location was in an area with a large concentration of Hispanic consumers. Knowing his cuisine wasn't necessarily going to attract the local crowd, he changed his eatery's name to Pizza Patrón and focused his marketing efforts on the Latino community.

It wasn't an easy decision for him to make. Swad—of Italian and Lebanese descent—was completely unversed in Latino culture when he made the strategic decision to pursue that market. To attract Latino customers, he hired bilingual employees for customer interaction positions, dedicated time and money to developing a large community service presence, and controversially, allowed customers to pay in pesos.[24] The shift in focus paid off—before Swad sold the business 30 years later, Pizza Patrón was a chain with 93 locations, all of them franchised.[25]

As the Pizza Patrón example demonstrates, demographics is a crucial external factor in business strategy. While it's not always possible or realistic for a company to change its DNA in response to its direct surroundings, it's imperative that business owners acknowledge that populations are always changing and keep those constant shifts in mind as their business progresses. To pick a few examples: Millennials are now a larger group than Baby Boomers, diversity is increasing, the middle class is shrinking, and Gen Xers are the veterans in the workforce.

Who are your customers right now? What needs do your products or services meet for them? What population or lifestyle shifts are occurring that will alter the significance and effectiveness of your offerings? And most importantly, what shifts on the horizon have the potential to impact your strategy?

The auto industry is going through material change: Internal combustion engines are under attack from electric challengers, escalating trade tensions are affecting global demand, the climate crisis has regulators fining companies that don't do enough to cut out carbon dioxide emissions,[26] and states are disagreeing with the federal government on miles per gallon standards with automakers in the middle or taking sides. But one of the biggest hurdles has been that services like Uber and Lyft are making car ownership optional. The prominent population that's contributed to this phenomenon? Millennials.

The fact that Millennials' hierarchy of needs is fundamentally different from previous generations has been well documented; they're putting off major purchases or avoiding them entirely. Chalk it up to student debt, low starting wages, struggling credit, or their rumored fear of commitment and then mix in the traffic and parking hassles in the urban areas where Millennials prefer to live, and the result is that car ownership among 18- to 34-year-olds has dropped by 30 percent in the past five years.[27] Where previous generations devoted a part of their monthly income to car payments, Millennials are prioritizing experiences over things—access over ownership. This reality has not only given rise to ride-sharing companies but also to car-sharing ones as well. Think Airbnb for cars.

Startups like Turo and Getaround allow drivers to rent cars from private car owners, and owners to rent out their cars for payment, for as short a period as a day. Big-time companies like Avis, U-Haul, and General Motors have their own car-sharing versions with subsidiaries Zipcar, UhaulCarShare, and Maven, respectively, that offer cars that can be rented for as little as an hour. Both options allow drivers to bypass a rental agency, a dealership-lease situation, or auto loan debt, and both are causing headaches for carmakers and lenders. And like Uber versus the taxi industry before them, this fight is a clash between an old-school business model and a modern technology platform inspired by the sharing economy—which the Millennial lifestyle embraces.

Subscription services are the newest arrival to the auto industry, which is exactly how it sounds: Sign up for the car you want, and cancel when you're done. This alternative option falls somewhere between renting a car for a day and signing a traditional three-year lease. A startup called Fair is one such subscription service, and it's done completely through an app. Drivers can get on their phones, choose a used vehicle, get pre-approved—Fair says it's not solely dependent on credit score, often good news for Millennials who don't have established credit—and complete the transaction within minutes. All the cars are located on nearby dealer lots, and Fair acquires the vehicle once a customer selects it. Fair then enters into a month-to-month agreement with the driver who subscribed to the car. They've begun seeing competition from fellow startups and car giants alike—BMW, Volvo, Jaguar Land Rover, Mercedes-Benz, Porsche, and Audi have all released similar subscription-like services, albeit with varied structures and a far heftier price tag.

The surge of car-sharing services, and the new business model they represent, came as a direct response to a shifting demographic trend, one that, as I mentioned, also includes the growth of urban populations and the subsequent rise of traffic. The companies within the market that observed and honored those shifts are the ones that are doing well (though some were just better positioned), and the ones that didn't are losing out on growth opportunities. The same can be said for many businesses in markets impacted by demography—like this next one.

Despite a US population growth rate that's at its lowest since 1937, consistent movement West has resulted in a very high population density and an exceptionally congested urban environment in some major cities. Among the numerous other ramifications that come along with overcrowding is a full-fledged housing crisis in California.

The 2018 national census numbers showed that the San Francisco Bay Area had over 800,000 residents, yet only 400,000 housing units.[28] An even more concerning ratio is Los Angeles County, which had over 10 million residents and only about 3.5 million housing units.[29] Not enough housing plus too many people equals an unrealistic value set on real estate, leading to hugely inflated purchase prices, astronomically high rent, and homelessness. Experts say that California needs to double its current rate of housing production (which is at about 100,000 per year) just to keep up with expected population growth and to prevent prices from further increasing. California also needs to quadruple the current rate of housing production over the next seven years in order for prices and rents to decline.[30]

In the meantime, a company called PodShare, which was founded by Moscow-born Elvina Beck, is helping make up for the shortage of affordable housing by building and renting out dormitory-style lodging in San Francisco and throughout Los Angeles. The buildings are communal, meaning people sleep in a bunk bed among other "pod-estrians" and share lounge areas, bathrooms, and a kitchen. There's no deposit and no commitment. Tenants can pay by the night, week, or month and get a bed (with a personal TV), a locker, access to Wi-Fi, food staples like cereal and ramen, and toiletries like toothpaste and toilet paper. The only thing not included is privacy. But considering tenants are only paying around $1,000 for a month's stay—slightly lower than the national median price of a one-bedroom apartment ($1,216 as of 2019), but *far* lower than a one-bedroom in San Francisco ($3,600) or Los Angeles ($2,230)[31]— they'd likely tell you that lack of privacy is a small price to pay.

The effects of demographic trends are everywhere, and on one level or another, affect many business strategies. Baby Boomers who want to remain active, combined with trends I've mentioned like big city urban traffic, are some of the factors behind the growth of electric bikes with companies like Rad Power Bikes. As older populations are growing (the 75- to 81-year-old contingent is growing 4 percent per year for the next five years, and the 82- to 86-year-old cohort begins to grow over 3 percent per year after 2019) the assisted living sector is growing.[32] Hispanics are projected to be the largest racial or ethnic minority group in the US electorate when voters cast their ballots in 2020, and that trend will impact the strategy of many politicians and businesses.[33] I can appreciate that thinking about who your customers are, what they're experiencing, and how that might be changing can be a really low priority amid the daily chaos of overseeing sales, accounting, hiring, and technology, but if a company is ignoring demographic changes in their market, it means they're not paying attention to their future.

ECONOMIC AND ENVIRONMENTAL

The fourth factor represented in TIDES is a double feature: economic and environmental. We'll start with economics, which is, simply put, how society deals with the production, distribution, and consumption of goods and services. To whittle it down even further, it's the state of the economy. Is it healthy? What's the current gross domestic product (GDP) growth rate? Is there too much inflation or deflation? What's the unemployment forecast? Where are interest rates currently set?

The US economy was in shambles after the subprime mortgage crisis of 2008. The stock market plummeted, banks became very conservative about giving out loans, and a number of interesting startups and alternative businesses launched as a consequence. One of those was Prosper Marketplace, the first-ever peer-to-peer online lending marketplace, which allowed individuals to either invest in personal loans or request to borrow money.

As an online business without physical banks, Prosper was not saddled with the cost structure of traditional banks. Even more important,

Prosper's peer-to-peer model was a way to circumvent the traditional bank or financial institution—it cut out the middleman, loosened eligibility requirements, provided quicker turnaround times for loan approval, and opened the pool of potential investors to those who looked at more than the borrower's credit score (although that too). Plus, it reduced risk. With each loan Prosper made, many different investors could chip in $25 or more, and the risk that a borrower wouldn't repay the loan was spread across many investors.

Prosper initially operated a variable rate model, like an eBay-style online auction marketplace with lenders and borrowers ultimately determining loan rates using a Dutch auction-like system—that is, where you start with a high asking price and work your way down. After they ran into regulatory opposition from the US Securities and Exchange Commission (SEC), they filed their first prospectus with the SEC and adopted preset rates based on a formula evaluating each prospective borrower's credit risk. That goes to show how just because a company was formed in order to take advantage of a flailing economy doesn't mean it's immune from having to shift with it; it also shows how TIDES factors can be interconnected, like institutional and economic are here.

Prosper's online lending marketplace eventually expanded to offer ten kinds of loans, from debt consolidation to small business to engagement ring financing. Borrowers can apply for loans ranging from $2,000 to $40,000, and investors can search for loans to diversify their portfolios based on loan category, amount, size of return, or length of term. So far, more than $16 billion has been loaned to more than 960,000 people.[34] It is a very effective business model and why, not surprisingly, peer-to-peer lending is also central to other online lenders such as LendingClub, Funding Circle, Upstart, CircleBack Lending, and Peerform. Clearly, peer-to-peer lending has successfully taken hold as a new option for consumers or small businesses needing loans and investors who want to lend to them.

Environmental, the bonus double-featured "E" in TIDES, hinges on the ecological and epidemiological impacts to a company's strategy—epidemics, pandemics, disease, natural disasters, weather, climate, and pollution. Some of these conditions can be forecasted, plotted, and in some cases, counteracted. Others happen slowly and can only be recognized over time, and still others happen extremely quickly and require swift strategy changes, such as the coronavirus (Covid-19) pandemic, which has caused catastrophic consequences around the world and is a riptide that is difficult to adapt to. The pandemic is developing just as this book is going to press, so please refer to my website, bradchase.net, for some strategy thoughts, lessons, and insights regarding Covid-19.

Agriculture is a critical sector of the US economy that is impacted by these environmental conditions. The crops, livestock, and seafood produced in the United States contribute billions to the economy each year, and when food-service and other agriculture-related industries are included, the agricultural and food sectors contribute over $1 trillion to the GDP.[35] If environmental conditions get extreme, they can wreak havoc on the health and yield of plants and threaten the global food supply.

One of those environmental extremes is the release of carbon dioxide (CO_2). Our climate crisis is primarily a problem of too much CO_2 in the atmosphere, and while we've all heard the enormous outputs that the energy sector emits through the combustion of fossil fuels, some environmental experts say agricultural farming emits 25 to 35 percent of all CO_2 into the atmosphere—more than all modes of transportation combined.[36]

To help farmers decrease their carbon footprint, a Boston-based agricultural technology startup called Indigo Agriculture unveiled a first-of-a-kind program to tackle climate change worldwide: a non-GMO seed treatment that captures and stores atmospheric carbon dioxide inside the soil instead of being automatically released into the air. The treatments consist of naturally occurring microbes, like plant-friendly bacteria and fungi, which are applied to seeds as a spray or powder coating before planting. Not only will this positively impact the environment, but it will also help farm profitability and crop nutrition.

Indigo's goal is to capture one trillion metric tons (a teraton) of carbon dioxide worldwide, and to catalyze the initiative, they offered incentives: $15 per metric ton of carbon dioxide sequestered (IndigoAg uses its digital agronomy capabilities and software imagery analysis to measure and verify soil carbon sequestration and on-farm emission levels); a nationwide sequestration competition where first-place growers receive a monetary prize; and a series of challenges to develop technologies for maximizing soil carbon sequestration rates, improving soil carbon measurements, and reducing the need for chemical and fertilizer inputs—winning innovations are awarded $1 million contracts.

In the face of environmental factors, companies like Indigo are trying to change the problem; their strategy centers around innovation, proficiency, and counteraction, and their incentives encourage a common good mentality—that is, that everyone align business practices toward becoming carbon neutral. Other companies are more focused on the result; it's not about how they can offset poor environmental conditions as much as it is about how they can make the best of them.

The Netherlands, about twice the size of New Jersey, one of the world's most densely populated countries, and one of the most flood-prone places in the world, almost never floods and doesn't bother with flood insurance even though much of the country is below sea level. Why? Because the Dutch allocate more than a billion dollars a year toward state-of-the-art innovation, blending form and function to protect its citizens from floods. A billion a year might seem like a lot, but consider that Hurricanes Katrina and Harvey cost a staggering $161 billion and $125 billion respectively. Hurricane Maria inflicted $90 billion in damage and Sandy another $65 billion.[37] And those are only four of a long list of costly damaging Atlantic hurricanes.

Some of the Dutch infrastructure is massive, like the Maeslantkering storm surge barrier, one of the largest moving structures on earth. Controlled by a supercomputer, it automatically closes when Rotterdam is threatened by floods. Rotterdam also has a basketball court that can hold 450,000 gallons of storm runoff, a sloping park atop a shopping center that also serves as a storm surge barrier, and a world-class rowing facility that doubles as a flood reservoir. The beach town of Katwijk was vulnerable to floods until Dutch engineers created natural-looking 25-foot-high dunes that protected the town from a sea surge or a big storm. The project also helped unclog streets as the engineers built a 700-space garage under the dunes to handle parking when tourists flock to the beach.[38]

Speaking of tourists, the tourism industry is greatly affected by environmental factors. The sector as a whole is entrenched in seemingly inescapable issues that affect businesses both directly and indirectly: sea-level rise and more acidic oceans threaten coastal tourism infrastructure and natural attractions; rising temperatures shorten winter sport seasons and threaten the viability of some ski resorts; climate change leads to changes in biodiversity, affecting ecotourism such as safari operators and wine vineyard tours; distributions of fish and other marine life change as the oceans warm, impacting recreational fishing and marine life watching.

Adaptation options exist, and the tourism sector has been using a diverse range of them, but many add costs to an already struggling industry and offer only short-term relief. Still, the businesses that strategically mine those gaps are the ones helping make a difference and staying afloat amidst the effects of Mother Nature.

Lake Tahoe, Nevada, is a prime spot for skiing and snowboarding in the winter and hiking in the summer, which results in about ten million cars coming in every year. To encourage visitors to rely less on private vehicles, the destination city improved public transportation systems by adding new buses, approximately half of which run on compressed natural gas.[39]

Most people don't shy away from the experience of staying at a resort, though some could argue that building and maintaining massive hotel resorts isn't an efficient use of existing resources nor is it an environmentally sustainable way to travel. Digital services like Airbnb and Vrbo tout the environmental benefits of home sharing, and in fact, an Airbnb-commissioned study says their guests "use 63 percent less energy than hotel guests."[40]

All of Royal Caribbean's ships now have purification systems that remove approximately 98 percent of sulfur dioxide emissions from its ship engines' exhaust, and the expedition cruise ship line Hurtigruten announced plans to have at least six ships powered by liquefied biogas—fossil-free, renewable fuel produced from dead fish and other organic waste.

The New York Hilton Midtown has a new 1.75 megawatt cogeneration plant powered by cleaner burning natural gas, which produces over 50 percent of the electricity and 35 percent of the steam needed to power the hotel's nearly 2,000 rooms and reduces the property's carbon footprint by more than 30 percent. Other Hiltons worldwide, of which there are more than 5,500, are installing energy-efficient lighting in guest rooms and public spaces and buying smart energy systems for kitchen vents and air-conditioning systems that turn off automatically when they're not in use.[41]

Tourism is both a victim of and a contributor to climate change. (A 2018 study found that tourism accounts for around 8 percent of global greenhouse gas emissions.[42]) And not least of which is due to the transportation to get where we're going. Newer planes have much more fuel-efficient engines, weight-saving features like lighter seats, and drag-reducing tweaks like upturned wings. Alaska Airlines is ranked as the most fuel-efficient domestic carrier[43] while Norwegian Air came in the highest for transatlantic routes.[44]

When it comes to economic and environmental factors, is your business strategy proactive or reactive? Will your company be the one to salvage the old or innovate the new? What parts of your strategy need to be deployed right now versus the short- and long-term?

SOCIAL

The final external factor in TIDES is social. This pertains to what's going on with consumer or business trends within specific industries. Social factors are mostly discretionary—meaning their importance is dictated by what's most influential for an individual company's success—and can include a broad range of things like comfort with technology, advertising preferences, buying habits, attitudes toward ecological products, fashion trends, and health consciousness. Tastes and trends are more fluid social influences than demographics because they reflect personal preferences, which are more likely to change on a whim.

Incorporating social factors into a business strategy all starts with knowing your target audience. How old are they? What are their lifestyle habits? What do they care about? How do they like to be communicated with? After answering these questions, you must then be intentional with how your offerings align with those factors and preferences, as well as how your product is being delivered, both from a marketing perspective and a distribution one.

Trends, by the very definition, are always changing, but the seriousness of some trends should not be underestimated. For example, a consumer preference for sustainability in everything from product sourcing to energy-efficient manufacturing is a trend that has proven to have staying power and is unlikely to change as environmental awareness continues to grow. Another is vegan eating. The global demand for plant-based food has become as much about animal welfare as it is about health, whether it's food allergies, celiac disease, lactose intolerance, lower rates of heart disease and cancer, or mindful weight loss. In the span of three years, there has been a 600 percent increase in people identifying as vegan in the United States alone, and Google Trends shows a huge worldwide increase in the interest in veganism (top regions include Israel, Australia, Canada, Austria, and New Zealand).[45] Companies like Impossible Foods and Beyond Meat are capitalizing on the global shift by making plant-based substitutes for meat products; the Impossible Burger is in over 5,000 restaurants in the United States, Hong Kong, Macao, and Singapore, and Beyond Burger is available at more than 35,000 locations, including the meat aisles in supermarkets.[46]

There are other trends, however, that are entirely dependent on circumstances. First-time mothers in the United States and other developed countries are older than ever.[47] The average age at which these women give birth now stands at 30 or above (US woman are younger than the average).[48] "Women are staying in school longer, they're going into the work force, they're waiting to get married, and they're waiting to have kids," according to John Santelli, a Columbia University professor of population.[49] Fertility rates are also changing. The global average fertility rate is just below 2.5 children per woman today, half of what it was 50 years ago. That is not surprising, as the modernization of societies generally reduces the number of kids women have.[50]

But what may surprise some people is that the fertility rate in the United States hit an all-time low in 2018[51] and that currently in the United States, about 10 percent of women—or 6.1 million—ages 15 to 44 have difficulty getting pregnant or staying pregnant.[52] As if that's not frustrating enough, traditional insurance has limited coverage for fertility care. In fact, only sixteen US states require insurers to either cover or offer coverage for infertility diagnosis and treatment, and of those, only ten have an insurance mandate that requires employers to include IVF (in vitro fertilization) coverage in their plans offered to employees.[53] Considering 155 million people in America get their healthcare benefits through their employers, this means there's an exorbitant number of people who are forced to pay out of pocket for fertility care.[54]

The growing cultural conversation on fertility is an important one in the ever-shifting healthcare landscape. Driving that conversation are factors like career aspirations, economic realities, and updated definitions of what a "traditional" family looks like. And it's not just what, but who. Today, there are females who want to preserve their fertility through egg freezing, LGBTQIA+ couples who use fertility treatments for family forming, and transgender individuals who seek to preserve future fertility options,[55] and the options currently available are slim to none.

In response, startups like Carrot Fertility are partnering with companies to provide fertility coverage for the millions of employees who need it—regardless of age, sex, sexual orientation, gender identity, or marital status. A fundamental part of Carrot's strategy is to make fertility care more accessible and affordable, which is why they take aim at the larger system and provide benefit packages for companies. They essentially have built their own system independent of carriers and the healthcare system as a whole; they process all reimbursements internally, validate claim details by the company's specific standards, and have their own platform that allows both employers and employees to manage their customized plans. It's a strong example of how cultural circumstances drive the need for adaptive change. And there are others.

Circa 2017, Stephen Colbert rocketed to the top of late-night talk show ratings. Even though *The Late Show* had premiered two years earlier, it had never exceeded the viewership that late-night competitors Jimmy Fallon or Jimmy Kimmel garnered. So how'd he do it? By catering his content to the many Americans who strongly disliked President Trump.

What's funny is that early criticism about the post-Letterman era was that Colbert's variety show dove too deeply into politics, as opposed to delving into silly games with celebrities like Fallon or creating shareable viral moments like Kimmel. But all of that changed when Donald Trump became president of the United States. Liberal viewers flocked to CBS to watch skits of actress Laura Benanti playing Melania Trump and interviews with Cartoon Trump who made regular appearances as a "guest" on the show, and Colbert made further headway by timing live episodes during the election and spending most of his monologue almost every night roasting the president.

A similar amount of intention and energy was applied by MSNBC, CNN, and Fox. Each of those networks know who their viewers are and what they want to consume and then cater to those different preferences. The more a business knows about the social trends that affect their community and industry, the better they'll be able to tailor their offerings to a shifting landscape.

Like the entertainment industry, retail is another where social trends play an extremely vital role. The last decade has seen a major social partiality to internet shopping; e-commerce has been a tidal wave that's completely transformed purchasing habits and business model infrastructure. Traditional retailers have found it harder to attract customers to their brick-and-mortar stores, resulting in locations being shut down and bankruptcies being filed.

As of 2019, e-commerce represented almost 10 percent of retail sales in the United States alone, with sales expected to hit $4.5 trillion in 2021.[56] Even though individual opinions vary and some statistics indicate a neck-and-neck race between Americans who prefer to shop online (51 percent) and those who would rather go to a store (the remaining 49 percent), e-commerce has a substantially faster growth rate than traditional retail: 15 percent compared to 5 percent.[57] That's not surprising when you consider society's sweeping desire for instant access, round-the-clock accessibility, and fast turnaround, and the disadvantages of the time required to shop in brick-and-mortar stores, transportation costs, parking hassles, and so on. For all those reasons and more, the digital world in which we live, and the online shopping that takes place in it, is fundamental to our economy.

Retailers closed a record 102 million square feet of store space in 2017, and then smashed that record in 2018 by closing another 155 million square feet. In 2019, more than 8,200 store closures were announced. Among them were popular chains like Sears, Party City, Walgreens, Barneys, Payless, Chico's, Gymboree, Kmart, Office Depot, and Pier 1 Imports.[58] Here's where this leaves the remaining brick-and-mortars: Go digital and/or get creative.

A prime example are independent bookstores, which were once endangered but are now seeing a resurgence. The number of independent bookstores has been growing every year since 2009, despite cheaper, more convenient ways to buy books online, in national chain stores, and with e-readers. Between 2009 and 2018, more than 800 independent bookstores opened up in the United States, bringing the total to more than 2,400—about a 49 percent jump after more than a decade of decline.[59] How did they do it? They refreshed their strategy.

Independent bookstores have a local appeal and a curated selection, but the profit margins on books are razor thin, so retailers often beef up their inventory with novelty items and in-store cafes, as well as draw crowds by hosting events—from book signings, readings, and live music to speed dating, literary costume contests, and even ukulele lessons (I couldn't make this stuff up)—which builds a much broader experience for customers. Buying a book becomes an act of community building as opposed to just a consumer purchase.

They also one-up the digital competition by providing better customer service. When's the last time you were shopping for a book online and had someone treat you like a friend and tell you about a niche book they love?

Indie bookstores may not have the cheapest and largest inventory, but they have far more latitude in choosing the salespeople who work there and which books they want to sell. What has emerged is a bifurcation of the industry where indie bookstores represent this individualized experience and a chance for the consumer to engage through a set of very personal dimensions, versus online book retailers that provide a book quickly, cheaply, and robotically.

Other brick-and-mortars have big expansion plans in the works, and those hinge on completely different, yet equally as ingenious, strategies. TJX, the retail company that owns stores like T.J. Maxx, Marshalls, and HomeGoods, opened 125 new stores in 2019 following 17 consecutive quarters of customer traffic increases.[60] In addition to their discount prices, their long-running success hinges on their varied mix of merchandise. It's a treasure-hunt, an eclectic and ever-changing mix of inventory, and a surprise on every aisle, and therein lies their secret weapon: a sense of urgency to commit and purchase, rather than just browse. It's there today but likely won't be there tomorrow, or ever again. Nordstrom made a bold bet opening its first flagship store in Manhattan at 57th and Broadway in late 2019. The 320,000-square-foot store spans four buildings and seven floors and offers 100,000 pairs of footwear, 10,000 handbags and small leather goods, 10,000 tubes of lipstick, 6,000 pairs of jeans (160 styles in more than 100 washes), and seven bars and restaurants. Plus, the store boasts an augmented reality Lipstick Finder, an interactive Fragrance and Skincare Finder, and numerous in-store beauty services.[61]

Peloton, the upscale exercise brand known for their $2,000 internet-connected stationary bike and $4,000 treadmill, currently has around 100 showrooms worldwide. Their digital-first brand strategically uses these showrooms—which are outfitted with its various connected hardware—as places to teach prospective buyers about the equipment and services platform, and it's proven to be successful: Retail made up roughly 30 percent of their $800 million in sales in 2018.[62]

While we're on the subject of Peloton and social trends, it is impressive how many current trends they have tapped into—the streaming-subscription trend, the trend toward fitness with a quasi-spiritual twist, the trend toward luxury athletic options, the trend toward staying home, the rise of media and product convergence. Peloton taps into all of them. They designed an exercise bike with the fit and finish of an Italian sports car, stream live workout sessions to a built-in tablet for a monthly fee, and foster a supportive culture around the program. It's a deceptively simple strategy that checks enough social trend boxes to warrant the price tag.

Regardless of the specifics of the social trends that affect a business, companies will always operate in a changing environment. Even if a business has built its reputation on qualities such as consistency and longevity, customers may value these qualities differently in social and political climates that are increasingly less predictable. Whether a business changes rapidly in response to social trends or responds to them by cultivating consistency, it's important to know how social trends are evolving and how to respond to them with products and marketing strategies.

Ultimately, what do all the external factors we covered—technological, institutional, demographic, economic and environmental, and social—have to do with your business strategy? Everything.

Over time, there will always be technological advancements or shortages, changes in legal or governmental regulations, demographic shifts in population or lifestyle, an economic boom or decline, environmental crises or progress, or prevalent social trends that are begging for capitalization. How your business adapts to all of these tides can mean the difference between success and failure.

141

CHAPTER 6

Expand the Universe

According to the Aspen Institute, nearly 50 percent of all US adults have worked in the restaurant industry at least once during their lives.[1] The stat's not too surprising considering there were over 1 million restaurants in the United States that generated sales of almost $900 billion in 2019 alone.[2] It's an enormous, lucrative, and heavily staffed industry, despite being one that has a high rate of failure. Statisticians fight over the exact number—many say 60 percent[3] of restaurants don't make it past their first year, while others report a more hopeful failure rate of 17 percent.[4] Regardless, there are countless challenges to building a successful restaurant business: location, food quality, service, managing costs, lots of competition, and the list goes on and on. And on top of all that, the restaurant industry is facing a seismic transformation. Mobile ordering, loyalty programs, cloud kitchens (which are set up only for online orders and have no location for dining in or picking up takeout), and digital delivery platforms are exploding.

Interestingly, when it comes to market potential, one of the biggest challenges is really basic: Restaurants have a limited physical capacity. They can only fit so many folks in the space. When you consider that 70 percent of restaurants in the United States only have a single location,[5] the scope of the problem magnifies—their universe is essentially limited to the confines of their building. For those restaurant owners who want to increase their revenues and profits, they must expand their universe by growing their customer base.

Consequently, restaurateurs have created franchises, happy hours, multiple locations (including food trucks), and focused on turning tables, catering, takeout, and food-delivery services. All these efforts help restaurateurs sell more food to more people, even in the face of space limitations.

Ezell's Chicken, a Seattle-based fast food chain, is a perfect example. Started over 35 years ago by Lewis Rudd and Ezell Stephens, Ezell's was a very popular takeout restaurant with fabulous fried chicken, amazing dinner rolls, and all the appropriate tasty side dishes. But when Oprah Winfrey was in town in 1989 and heard about Ezell's, she tried it, loved it, and mentioned it on her show. (She has since also had Ezell's FedExed to her in Chicago.) After that, Ezell's popularity exploded, the phone started ringing off the hook, and customers waited in line for hours. For three months, Ezell's could not cook enough chicken. Today, Ezell's is a Seattle institution that has expanded to 14 locations in the Seattle metropolitan area and is also known for giving back to the community.[6]

Expanding the universe is a simple, well-understood method for growing market potential. There are two basic approaches: increase your revenue and profits by delivering new products or price increases to your existing customers, or reach out to new customers with your current or, more often, new products that provide them added value.

Apple started out with one iPhone and now there are many. All these models help Apple reach more customers via a product lineup that has different price points and feature sets. And that has helped Apple grow its base of iPhone users. In early 2019, Apple said its installed base of iPhone users worldwide was 900 million, and at least one industry analyst predicts Apple will reach 1 billion active users in 2020. But overall the iPhone business continues to slow. As I mentioned earlier, users are holding on to their phones longer and competition has intensified. The growth of first-time smartphone buyers has also slowed.[7] The result? iPhone year-over-year revenues fell in Apple's 2019 Q3 and Q4.

But overall Apple's revenue was up because of the growth in its other businesses.[8] Apple has expanded its iPhone universe with a lot more than additional phones. They've added new hardware products, like the Apple Watch and AirPods, which operate hand in hand with the iPhone. Even the iPad and iPhone work better together than they do separately, giving users a reason to buy both. Apple has also expanded its universe with new services like Apple Music, the App Store, Apple Pay, Apple Card, Apple Arcade, and iCloud.

Expanding the universe to grow market potential is such a common and obvious strategic tactic that you see it every day without even thinking much about it: car companies adding new car models; Amazon starting as a bookseller before expanding over time to sell almost everything; Starbucks adding new drinks, seasonal drinks, and more locations;

airlines adding new routes; Coke adding new soft drinks and expanding into other drinks entirely when consumers wanted healthier alternatives.

PARTNERSHIPS

Forging partnerships is a common tactic that companies use to reach new customers or create new offerings. The Microsoft-IBM partnership I talked about at the beginning of the book worked for many years and helped IBM launch its successful PC while helping Microsoft reach customers it never would have reached otherwise. Ultimately, that partnership fell apart in dramatic fashion because the two companies' goals were very different over time, and without aligned goals partnerships never last.

Sonos and IKEA are collaborating on SYMFONISK, a range of Wi-Fi speakers designed to fit in your decor like home furnishings. They work with all the other Sonos speakers and integrate with the IKEA design aesthetic—for example, one SYMFONISK product is a table lamp that doubles as a great-sounding speaker. Sonos reaches new customers via new products and a new distribution partner, and IKEA has a new type of product to sell.

Sherwin-Williams and Pottery Barn are collaborating on an exclusive line of paint colors that has the same dynamic. Uber has partnered with Spotify and Pandora so riders can play the music they want from their Uber app when using the ride-sharing service—it gives Uber a small benefit over other ride-sharing options and helps Spotify and Pandora grow their streaming usage. Taco Bell's Doritos Locos Tacos feature a hard taco shell flavored with Doritos spices, and both companies benefit from new sales and powerful branding.

Mystified by the list of company names on the screen in the opening or ending credits of movies? That's because of the plethora of partnerships involved. A small production house will handle the filming and postproduction, and a larger studio will handle financing, marketing, and distributing the film. For example, J. J. Abrams' Bad Robot and Paramount Pictures have a partnership agreement,[9] and each expands its universe with the help of the other.

Airlines have banded together to form alliances that share routes, frequent flier miles, and so on. Delta SkyMiles program has around two dozen SkyMiles partners like KLM, Air France, and Aeromexico. Similarly, the Star Alliance is a global network of partners that include Lufthansa, United, Air Canada, Singapore Airlines, and many, many others. These partnerships help build loyalty with frequent fliers.

Video game manufacturers have always formed partnerships to help fund game development and promote games to help sell their consoles. In the past, video games tended to focus primarily on teenage boys, and the industry struggled to expand its universe beyond them, but in more recent years, partnerships like *Skylanders: SuperChargers* and race car driver Max Chilton, Marvel Studios and mobile game developer FoxNext (maker of *Marvel Strike Force*), and Google and Ubisoft (video game company behind *Assassin's Creed Odyssey*, which will be featured on Google's new Stadia gaming platform) substantially widened the nets of the video game industry to include new customers. This not only increased their volume of customers with more of the same demographic, but it also stretched their audience to include more ages, genders, ethnicities, and niche interest groups.

ADAPT TO CHANGE

Many times, especially in today's marketplace, progressing technology is what drives the need for and rate of expansion (video games being a prime example). But quite often, universe expansion is necessary because core markets and customers are changing. In this regard, ESPN provides an interesting case study. ESPN started as a cable sports station that, over the years, has added lots of original programming: *SportsCenter,* X Games, NFL Primetime, *30 for 30,* and *Outside the Lines* are just a handful of hundreds of examples. ESPN also signed deals with most of the major sports leagues to broadcast their games, including but by no means limited to Major League Baseball, the National Basketball Association, the National Football League, the National Hockey League, and college football and baseball.

Over time, they've added every type of media you can think of. It started with a website early on, and then a magazine, radio programming, and streaming, followed by more websites (like ESPN Deportes, The Undefeated, espnW, ESPN FC, X Games, SEC Network), sports fantasy leagues, and mobile apps. All these services reinforced ESPN as the leading sports media company, added more revenue, and "built tall walls" that made it harder for others to compete.

Their most recent big bet is ESPN+, a premium subscription service that costs $4.99 per month. As of the end of 2019, ESPN announced it had over 6.6 million subscribers for the new premium service[10] and expected 8 to 12 million subscribers by 2024.[11]

ESPN+ is particularly strategic to ESPN because the dynamics of watching television is changing. ESPN's major revenue source is the approximately $8 is gets per month from cable and satellite television companies every time someone subscribes to a cable TV package.

Though in 2017 ESPN still captured about one-third of sports viewing, ESPN's revenue from cable fees is decreasing because some consumers are "cutting the cord"—no longer subscribing to cable television because of the plethora of alternatives. According to the Disney annual report (Disney owns ESPN), ESPN lost 2 million subscribers, from 88 million to 86 million, during its 2018 fiscal year. ESPN's subscriber base has decreased about 14 percent since 2010—a revenue loss of hundreds of millions of dollars. ESPN+ needs to be successful if ESPN is to counter the loss of revenue in its traditional cable-satellite business.

Of course, the same trends impacting ESPN are impacting everyone in the media business. The ubiquity of broadband—a major technology change—is altering the fundamentals of the television and movie industries. Companies, one after the other, are expanding their services so that users can sign up to view their content without having a cable or satellite subscription: Disney's premium subscription service, called Disney+, features not only Disney content but also movies and television shows from other Disney-owned brands liked Star Wars, Pixar, Marvel, and National Geographic. Disney+ is priced, at least for now, at an aggressively low $6.99 a month. Disney also already owns the majority share of the streaming service Hulu (Comcast's NBCUniversal is also an equity stakeholder, owning 33 percent), which it will focus on more adult edgier shows; CBS has its own streaming service called CBS All Access; Showtime (owned by CBS) has the Showtime streaming service; HBO has HBO Now for users to watch HBO shows without a cable subscription; YouTube has YouTube TV; Roku has The Roku Channel.

The list of companies with a dream to stream seems endless. AT&T lost more than a million TV subscribers in the third quarter of 2019 from its cable and satellite (DirectTV) ventures. It was the seventh straight quarter in which AT&T lost more TV customers than it did in the quarter before.[12] To stem that tide, AT&T has a new HBO offering called HBO Max that will include shows from TBS and TruTV, and film studios, including Warner Bros., DC Films, and New Line. AT&T has stated publicly that the service could reach a whopping 50 million U.S. subscribers in its first five years.[13] Comcast /NBCUniversal has a streaming service called Peacock featuring popular shows like *The Office*, *Frasier*, and *Cheers*, and Apple has gotten in the streaming game too. And all of these services compete with heavyweights like Netflix, with its almost 170 million worldwide users, Amazon Prime, and many others, including good old-fashioned cable and satellite TV networks like CBS, NBC, ABC, USA, Univision, Discovery, and countless more. As technology and consumer habits change TV-viewing, old universes are shrinking, and media companies are having to expand into new ones.

Interestingly, the strategies behind this plethora of streaming services are different. While ESPN is trying to maintain and grow its media revenue and maintain its position as the leading media brand in sports, the goals of Amazon, Apple, and Roku for their streaming services are to expand other universes—services, devices, software, and other products. In 2016, Amazon's chief executive, Jeff Bezos, told journalist Walt Mossberg at Vox's Code Conference "when we win a Golden Globe, it helps us sell more shoes." AT&T hopes to grow its media revenue but also sell more wireless services and expand its digital advertising-data arm, Xandr, with the $109 billion it spent buying Time Warner. Disney+ hopes to use its streaming service not only for media revenue but to grow other Disney revenue streams like theme parks, merchandise, and cruises.[14]

Of course, when trying to reach new customers or old ones with new products, success is by no means guaranteed. Nike launched the FuelBand wristband fitness tracker to great fanfare in 2012 only to shut down the project four years later; they misjudged the market (ignoring Android users) and didn't have the expertise to build the hardware and software to compete with rivals like Fitbit and Jawbone. Nike is not alone in the challenges it faced in the wearables market. There have been other seismic changes. Jawbone went out of business in 2017. Fitbit had ups and downs and was eventually bought by Google for just over $2 billion in November 2019. The Apple Watch was initially a disappointment, but sales seem to be picking up (Apple does not break out Apple Watch sales, so it is hard to be sure). Garmin continues to be a strong player in the wearables market as well.

Amazon failed with its Kindle Fire phone after poor reviews cited things like inadequate design, zero cache, non-competitive pricing, and brazen attempts to lock its users into its own ecosystem of products by adding what amounted to a "buy" button on the side of the phone (click it, and you'd be that much closer to a two-day delivery).[15]

Target closed 133 stores, let go 17,000 employees, and lost billions of dollars after only two years of trying to expand into Canada; they didn't develop an effective supply chain before entering the Canadian market, and consequently, store shelves were poorly stocked. In addition, the chain reportedly didn't understand the competitive market and the shopping habits of Canadian customers.[16]

Google's smart glasses, Google Glass, and Google+ (Google's Facebook competitor) both failed because they didn't satisfy customers, and in the former case, the product raised safety and privacy concerns. Microsoft has made mistakes when trying to grow into new markets too. Microsoft came out with its own mobile operating system, Windows Mobile, in 2000. Apple debuted its iPhone in 2007, followed by Google's Android platform in 2008. While Microsoft had a mobile operating system well before Apple and Google, it fell victim to a poor product and business model and bad timing, and it quickly fell behind the competition. It never caught up and eventually exited the mobile operating system business altogether.

EXPANSION PLANS SHOULD BE CONSISTENT WITH YOUR STRATEGY

What these examples show is that no matter how many diverging paths you find, in the end, when a business tries to expand its universe, it succeeds or fails just like any other business—all on the merits of its strategy. How do customer value and execution compare to the competition? What is the market potential of the universe you are expanding into?

YETI cofounders Ryan and Roy Seiders were just two frustrated fishermen when they decided to reinvent the cooler back in 2006. The brothers didn't actually set out to reinvent it per se, they just wanted to design one that was heavy duty enough to withstand their fishing tactics—primarily, one they could stand on without fear of collapse as they sight-casted for redfish. And, of course, they wanted it to look cool and keep their drinks cold during a full day on the water.

They produced a prototype using a rotomolding process, the same process used to make kayaks and those orange plastic barriers you pass on the road. It involved pouring a powdered polyethylene plastic resin into a mold and creating one dense shell, as opposed to putting together smaller components. The result was a seamless, insulated, and nearly indestructible product that managed insanely high ice retention. The only problem? Due to the high manufacturing cost, they realized they'd have to sell their cooler at retail for about $300 a pop. No such market existed.

At the time, most coolers were made by Igloo or Coleman or Rubbermaid, and the largest ones cost somewhere in the mid-double digits at big-box retailers like Walmart and Target. The brothers knew they'd have to find a new distribution path. Convinced that outdoorsman like them would value a high-quality product enough to pay a premium for it, they called on hardware and tackle shops and offered this proposition: Why try to compete with Walmart selling $30 coolers and keep the $5 margin when you can sell a $300 cooler and keep $100?

YETI's sales hit $5 million in 2009, and as word continued to spread among the hardcore "hook and bullet" crowd, they closed in on $29 million in 2011. Still, in 2013, they did a brand tracking study that showed just 4.4 percent awareness among their core outdoor audience. So as a marketing tactic, the Seiders brothers reached out to well-known fishers and hunters for testimonials. But because they didn't have the funds to sponsor their famous spokespeople, they offered free coolers in exchange for video testimonials. Industry professionals got a free cooler out of the deal, and the brand slowly started strengthening its credibility. It was a win-win.

Around the same time, YETI mindfully expanded their distribution model to include natural tangents to hunting and fishing, like rural feed-and-seed stores that targeted farmers and ranchers who worked and played outside and liked to barbeque, as well as outdoor recreation retailers, like REI, that targeted campers who surely valued durability and still-cold food and drinks. YETI sales hit $147 million that year.[17]

With their distribution model locked and loaded, they began expanding their product line. They started with a portable, over-the-shoulder soft cooler called the Hopper. Not to be outdone by any other soft cooler on the market, this one featured four tie-down points, insulating material that made it buoyant, and a zipper borrowed from cold-water survival suits that made the cooler watertight. Then they created drinkware that featured vacuum-insulated stainless steel that keeps hot drinks hot and cold drinks cold for eons, backpacks that were puncture and abrasion resistant, and chairs that had cast joints like the ones used on truck door hinges. By 2015, YETI was a gotta-have-it label synonymous with premium quality, and their sales skyrocketed to $468 million. In 2018, they hit $778 million.[18]

What started as a niche, one-product company grew into a mass-market, high-end, durable, innovative brand for outdoorsmen, tailgaters, and backyard barbecuers everywhere. YETI wisely started by executing well on its original bet by first building a high-quality, indestructible cooler and prioritizing the right distribution channels, finding ones that aligned with their passionate commitment to the outdoors and their target demographic of outdoor enthusiasts. Then they were smart about publicity, widening their reach through grassroots marketing and relying on a small group of credible people to spread the word. Finally, they were smart about their product and business evolution, expanding their universe to include options that were purposeful and in keeping with their operating philosophy of quality over quantity.

The order in which they did all of these things was paramount. By initially establishing appropriate channels and then slowly introducing products in new categories, they were able to expand to a broader customer base while increasing their sales to people already familiar with the brand. It was an intentional rollout of compounding effects—one that can teach us a lot about healthy expansion.

MERGERS & ACQUISITIONS

Most of the universe expansion examples cited in this chapter so far are internal: A company like YETI adding new products to grow its customer base, revenue, and profits. Of course, another means of universe expansion is via mergers and acquisitions. The magnitude of deals is stunning. According to the Institute of Mergers, Acquisitions and Alliances, since 2000, more than 790,000 transactions have been announced worldwide with a known value of over $57 trillion. In 2018 alone, there were 49,000 worldwide transactions valued at $3.8 trillion. The largest in the United States in 2018 was health insurer Cigna Corporation acquiring Express Scripts Holding, the largest pharmacy benefit manager in the United States, in December 2018 for almost $68 billion. In early 2019, Bristol-Myers Squibb announced an even larger healthcare acquisition, buying cancer drugmaker Celgene in a cash and stock deal valued at $74 billion.[19] Disney has acquired a boatload of media content including Pixar (2006, $7.4 billion), Marvel (2009, $4 billion), Lucasfilm for the Star Wars franchise (2012, $4.06 billion), and 21st Century Fox (2017, $84 billion)[20] to name just a few of its many acquisitions.

The list of megadeals goes on and on, but naturally, not all transactions are multibillion-dollar deals. The Piston Group was started as a suburban Detroit auto parts business in 1995 by then newly retired NBA champion Vinnie Johnson of the Detroit Pistons. The original goal of the company was to bring jobs and opportunity, as well as economic vitality, to Detroit through the assembly of auto-related products like powertrain cooling systems, chassis, battery packs, and interiors. It hit $1.3 million in sales during its first year of business, mainly because of a contract with General Motors (GM)—the result of Johnson cold calling Harold Kutner, GM vice president of global purchasing in the 1990s, after reading in a newspaper that he vowed to support companies willing to open in Detroit with jobs.[21]

Over the next few years, Piston Group became an MBE certified, minority-owned business enterprise (which requires a company to be at least 51 percent minority-owned, operated, and controlled) and got the necessary certifications required in the auto industry for environmental performance, defect prevention, and quality assurance. Several new products hit the assembly line, along with new and innovative test methods, all of which led to another important contract, with Ford Motor Company. Piston Group was well on its way to making a name for itself.

In the early 2000s, Piston Group acquired AIREA, an office design studio and furniture dealer with stores in Detroit and Southfield, Michigan, and turned it into a soup-to-nuts commercial interiors company that fit under the Piston Group banner. By 2010, company-wide sales hit $326 million and it had 241 employees, up from the initial 20.

A short time later, Piston Group acquired Detroit Thermal Systems, a manufacturer of climate control systems and components, and come 2015, the company did $1.2 billion in sales, had 1,367 employees, and boasted a customer list that included Detroit's Big Three (General Motors, Ford Motor Company, and Fiat Chrysler Automobiles) as well as Honda, Toyota, and Nissan.[22]

But its biggest expansion (at least so far) came in 2016 through the acquisition of Irvin Automotive, a Detroit supplier of interior trim and seating components. That purchase strengthened Piston Group's engineering and manufacturing expertise, allowed them to provide a concept-to-completion platform for the first time, added more than 8,000 employees to their workforce, and brought in a string of new customers, including Black Diamond, Golden Technologies, Delta, and Southwest Airlines.[23]

Their universe did more than expand; it exploded. As of 2019, Piston Group had 19 facilities that spanned from Michigan to Mexico, amounting to more than 2.3 million square feet of cumulative workspace. They employed over 10,000 people, worked on more than 35 vehicle platforms, and earned $2.88 billion in revenue during the last reported fiscal year.[24]

Acquisitions were key to Piston Group's growth and allowed them to expand into new services, new areas of expertise, and new distribution channels, all of which led them to securing new customers. It's a great example of using acquisitions as a core method to expand one's universe and achieve continuous growth.

I know it is corny, but when you think about how to grow your market and expand your universe, think about how big the universe is, where it's best for your company to go, and the best routes your spaceship can take to get there. Sometimes you want a moonshot, but sometimes you just need to go down the street a little . . .

CHAPTER 7

Climb Short Walls;
Build Tall Walls

Did you know there are over 11,000 drugs in the global market?[1] Pharmaceuticals is nearly a trillion-dollar industry ($982 billion in 2018, to be exact[2]), with hundreds of companies around the world discovering, developing, producing, and marketing drugs for all the different things that plague the human body. Of those hundreds of companies, Pfizer is one of the largest. And by largest, I mean product volume, number of patient prescriptions, name recognition, and total revenue.[3]

Pfizer was founded by German American Charles Pfizer after he and his cousin produced an antiparasitic treatment in 1849. But the production of citric acid in the 1880s is what really put Pfizer on the map; the company went from working out of a small brick building to buying the block the building sat on and expanding it into a lab and factory. By 1906, their sales exceeded $3 million, and they had nearly 200 employees.[4]

In the century to follow, they developed and mass-produced penicillin and Terramycin (antibiotics), Feldene (an anti-inflammatory that became their first product to reach one billion dollars in total sales), Zoloft (antidepressant), Glucotrol (diabetes medication), Zithromax (for fighting bacterial infections), Viagra (erectile dysfunction), and Xalkori (cancer), among countless others.[5] But it was Lipitor, the cholesterol medication and best-selling drug in the history of pharmaceuticals,[6] that established Pfizer as an uncontested pharmaceutical powerhouse.

Lipitor was originally synthesized by Warner-Lambert—a midsized drugmaker best known for consumer health products like Listerine mouthwash, Benadryl allergy pills, and Halls cough drops—in 1985. Back then, the public was just starting to learn what cholesterol was. There was little evidence that controlling it with medication could be so crucial in preventing disability and early death, and the coming epidemic of obesity and diabetes in an aging population wasn't foreseen. It was with that mindset that doctors and the four other established manufacturers of statins, the class of drugs that lowers bad cholesterol (LDL), dismissed Lipitor as an unnecessary market addition and nonviable contender.

It wasn't until 1990, when Warner-Lambert began putting the medication through clinical trials, that everything changed. The results from the initial round of testing showed that the drug tremendously out-performed the other statins; it worked as well at its lowest dose as the others did at their highest. What's more, early studies showed that the drug might also help people with heart problems, diabetes, and stroke risk by reducing the buildup of plaque in the arteries. Pfizer approached Warner-Lambert about a partnership, offering to help fund the expensive late-stage testing of the drug and promote Lipitor after it launched. Together, they patented the drug, and upon official approval by the FDA for medical use, it hit the market in 1997. Within the first 12 months, it reached $1 billion in domestic sales. Pfizer bought out Warner-Lambert in 2000, and over the next 14 years, Pfizer raked in over $125 billion on Lipitor sales alone.[7]

To understand just how high the wall was that Pfizer built around their blockbuster drug, we have to first touch on the significance of patents. By definition, patents are a type of intellectual property right that provides protection over an invention. In this case, the invention was Lipitor, and once it was patented, no one else could create, use, manufacture, or sell it without Pfizer's approval (which, of course, was never granted).

Drug patents typically last for 20 years, so in the meantime, a common work-around for outside drug manufacturers is to produce generic versions of the drug—that is, copying a brand-name drug to have exactly the same dosage, effects, and strength as the original and then selling it at a cheaper cost. Pfizer saw this coming a mile away, so in addition to the patent, they also applied for and were granted exclusivity over Lipitor; they protected their drug from all generic drug competition. They were alone in the market, surrounded by their very own indestructible and unscalable wall.

Of course, both the patent and exclusivity would one day expire, but that had little bearing on Pfizer's dominance of the statin market over the course of the next decade. Lipitor garnered tens of millions of prescriptions, peaked at $12.8 billion in sales in a single year, and consistently accounted for about a quarter of Pfizer's annual revenue.[8] By the time the patent expired, at the end of 2011, Pfizer was the most lucrative pharmaceutical company in the world.[9]

In the field of pharmaceuticals, patents are a form of monopoly that provide the protection of tall, impenetrable walls. And while they don't last forever, they're an effective way to keep competitors at bay while the manufacturer profits on the research that went into coming up with the drug in the first place. Pfizer's revenue has taken a hit since the patent expiration (though they've still averaged about $52 billion annually thanks to their plethora of other prescription drugs[10]), and they may never be able to duplicate the heyday of their Lipitor success, but their tall wall in the form of a patent was something they took advantage of for many years, and it established them as a pharmaceutical giant.

"Climb Short Walls; Build Tall Walls" is all about barriers to entry, an imperative concept to employ when building a business or entering a new market. When walls are short, it is easier to enter or compete in a market. On the other hand, tall walls provide loyalty, defense, and security. You want to build your business in such a way that it isn't easy for someone else to compete, and you do so by creating conditions or circumstances that put your company in a superior business position. Now in most cases, you do that the old-fashioned way with great products or customer service or attractive prices, and so forth, that earn loyalty from customers. Those are the essential fundamentals. But, in addition, there are common practices that can help some businesses extend their wall even higher. Pfizer built a patent tall wall with Lipitor, but there are many additional tall wall approaches you can take.

EXECUTION TALL WALLS

There are an endless number of tall walls that can be built through execution. Get the right locations for your business and it becomes that much harder for your competitors to compete. If you hire special talent and find people with the right expertise, it will make things tougher for your competitors. (This is especially true when talent is committed with an employment contract, like in professional sports where owners sometimes sign long-term contracts with key players.) The partnership strategy I discussed in the last chapter can not only increase revenue and customers, and it can also build taller walls, like it did for Warner-Lambert and Pfizer. Access to a limited supply chain, superior manufacturing, and hard-to-replicate product design are additional examples of execution tall walls.

Sometimes you can build a business model tall wall and a strategic advantage by exploiting a weakness a competitor can't easily respond to. As mentioned earlier, other streaming companies can't compete with the broader advantages of Amazon Prime and Amazon in general. Similarly, Tesla choosing to sell cars direct via the web is something traditional car dealers cannot easily do because of their long history and investments in their car dealer channels. Apple is not an advertising company and can be more virtuous with its privacy policies with the iPhone than Google, who depends on user data from Android phones to personalize ads and maximize advertising revenue. Conversely, Google as an advertising company could offer its Android phone operating system for free to phone makers because Google benefits from the data where as Microsoft did not have that advantage when it tried to sell its early Windows phone operating system to handset makers.

PRODUCT TALL WALLS

Products can be tall wall products because their design and use inherently builds tall walls. Take major machinery or any system critical to the operations of a business, such as enterprise software products like SAP, Salesforce, Workday, Oracle, and many others that run core business operations like accounting, procurement, human resources, project management, sales, and supply chain operations. Because of their cost and/or learning curve and/or integration with key business processes, once these products are integrated into a business, it is nontrivial to change them.[11]

Nespresso is another very different example. Nespresso has reimagined the razor-razor blade strategy I mentioned earlier—wherein one item is sold at a low price (razor) in order to increase sales of a complementary good (razor blade)—Nespresso sells both its espresso machines and the specialty coffee pods that go with them for a premium price, but the machines and the pods make a very good cup of coffee quickly and easily and are popular with customers. The pairing of machine and pod means one is reliant on the other, even more so while both the Nespresso machines and coffee capsules were under patent (in 2010, they had 1,700 of them protecting them from competitors).[12] But as they've expired, a slew of machines and Nespresso-compatible pods have entered the market.

That said, those machines often can't compete with Nespresso's upper segment marketing strategy with George Clooney as the company spokesperson, nor do competitors' pods offer the "hermetically sealed" capsule made of aluminum that keeps the coffee aroma from degrading. So in addition to the original patents, Nespresso built tall walls and has brewed a massive cup of cash through an excellent product, the machine-consumables business model, direct sale systems-distribution model (more than 10 million online capsule subscribers, 700 carefully staged boutiques in 67 countries[13]), and a compelling, well-respected brand.

Sonos is yet another example. The pioneer of wireless audio systems faces stiff competition on the low end with smart, voice-activated speakers from folks like Amazon and Google, but Sonos makes superior-sounding speakers that can stream audio from your favorite streaming services as well as enhance the audio from TVs. And once you get a couple of Sonos speakers, it becomes natural to extend the system throughout your home by adding more speakers. Need to add another room? Add a couple more speakers. Need better-sounding audio for your flat-screen TV? Add a Sonos sound bar. And because of the product design, it's easy to add these new speakers and play the music you want in whatever room or multiple rooms you want. Once you have a couple of Sonos speakers, it's much less likely you will move to a competitor.

Apple has built product tall walls too. Even though Android-based phones are excellent, many customers will never switch from their iPhone. Why? Because they use iMessage to text with friends and family, and iMessage has advantages over traditional text messaging. iPhones users lament texting with Android users or being a part of group chats that include Android users because not all the iMessage features work on Android phones. Of course, Android users have a similar reaction, only in reverse. There are other iMessage features liked by iPhone users. Many iPhone users seem enraptured with iMessage blue bubbles that indicate a text message is sent from another iPhone user. If you don't know it already, the iMessage green bubbles indicate an Android user is texting you. iMessage gives a visual cue when someone is drafting a message back to you, it has end-to-end encryption to protect privacy, longer message support, and better support for effects and stickers and graphics.

Some customers use FaceTime to communicate with friends and family, and like iMessage, FaceTime is only available on the iPhone. Or maybe they share photo albums on Apple's iCloud, and that makes it harder to switch phones. Or maybe they use an Apple Watch, Apple Music, and AirPods, which all work seamlessly with the iPhone. You get the picture. (And, as I discussed earlier, this ecosystem of Apple's add-on products for the iPhone is a way that Apple expands the universe to bring in more revenue, so they get a strategic double whammy.) And to throw one more iPhone product tall wall at you, Apple makes it super easy to upgrade to a new iPhone from an older one. Upgrading from an iPhone to an Android-based phone is more difficult.

BRAND TALL WALLS

Apple, Nespresso, and Sonos have built powerful brands to go along with the tall wall design inherent in their product design. Building a successful brand requires a thoughtful combination of product, marketing, and customer insight, but if customers know your brand, trust your brand, and maybe even identify themselves with your brand, your brand can help build tall walls.

Spanx is a shapewear empire with an estimated $400 million in yearly sales,[14] but in 1998, founder Sara Blakely was a 20-something who sold fax machines door-to-door. The panty hose she was required to wear were uncomfortable and old-fashioned, and she hated the way the seamed foot stuck out of open-toed shoes, but she loved the control-top. So she cut the feet off of a pair and wore them underneath some slacks. When the ends of the panty hose kept rolling up her legs, she knew what she needed to do: create an undergarment that didn't exist.

Blakely spent two years and her entire $5,000 savings meticulously planning her product. She visited craft stores to find the right fabrics for her prototype. She sought out hosiery mills and started cold calling. She researched every hosiery patent ever filed and, to save $3,000 in legal fees, wrote her own patent for Footless Body-Shaping Pantyhose with the help of a textbook bought at Barnes & Noble. She convinced buyers from Neiman Marcus to test the Spanx product in several stores, and soon, Bloomingdale's, Bergdorf Goodman, and Saks followed suit. If she wasn't at one of the stores posing as a customer to bait shoppers to buy Spanx, she was at the department store staff meetings showing sales associates why Spanx shouldn't be in the isolated world of hosiery but sold alongside womenswear and shoes.[15]

And little by little, the wall got taller.

Blakely sent Spanx samples to Oprah Winfrey's stylist, and Winfrey chose it as her favorite product of the year on her annual Favorite Things Show (no advertising in the world can match a seal of approval like that). She scored a coveted deal with QVC and sold 8,000 pairs of Spanx in the first six minutes.[16] The Spanx product line expanded to include maternity pantyhose, slimming apparel, and bras, and the company went international by launching in the UK and Australia. It got its own shop inside an NYC Bloomingdale's, followed by its first-ever standalone store in Virginia.[17] By 2012, Spanx offered over 200 products in 40 countries.[18]

Since its inception, a long list of Spanx competitors have flooded the market, but with the support of tall walls, Spanx has continued its leadership. Spanx has patent tall walls like Pfizer had with Lipitor. The company has 30 patents[19] and a top-notch legal team that's unrelenting in its pursuit of patent or trademark copycats. Spanx's distribution has also been a key part of its tall walls. As of 2019, its products—which now include menswear, swimwear, denim, and accessories—were sold in tens of thousands of department stores, boutiques, and online shops across 65 countries[20] and 20 standalone Spanx retail stores in the United States.[21] But perhaps its more important tall wall is its brand tall wall. Spanx is to slimming undergarments what Kleenex is to tissues or Google is to search: a brand that stands for the category. That type of brand recognition can't be purchased; it's beyond valuable. Brand tall walls give companies like Spanx a leg up over their competition because customers trust their products and the companies that make them.

Many companies have powerful brand tall walls like Spanx. Brooks makes superior running shoes and is a brand runners trust. Starbucks, Nordstrom, Uniqlo, Rolex, Dunkin' Donuts, Disney, Nike, Dyson, The Red Cross, Microsoft, Harley-Davidson, Cisco, Caterpillar, and many other companies also have strong brands. Products and not just companies can have powerful brands that help build tall walls. Think of Tylenol, Tide, Pampers, Colgate, and Lay's to name just a few.

But you don't have to be a national company to build your brand. Tom Douglas is one of a number of well-known chefs in the Seattle area who owns and operates numerous restaurants, has a catering arm, and sells food products. Tom has built a local brand through great food, impressive philanthropic efforts, media efforts like cooking shows, and his reputation as a great person to work for. Though it's hard to build tall walls in the restaurant business, Tom's is a little higher because of his brand.

MARKETING TALL WALLS

Sometimes consumer loyalty can be increased with marketing programs—tall walls lengthened through loyalty programs. Credit card points give you value as a customer and make it less enticing for you to switch cards. Hotel chains promote loyalty by giving you points for staying with them. Stores like Starbucks, CVS, Bed Bath & Beyond, Kohl's, Best Buy, and Nordstrom give you points for buying from them. Ever hear of someone taking a crazy flight at the end of the year just to have a certain status with an airline frequent flier program? Those programs build tall walls and encourage fliers to be loyal to those airlines.

A cousin of loyalty programs is membership programs. Amazon Prime costs over $100 a year, but all its benefits—rapid delivery options; free streaming movies, television shows, and music; Kindle owners' lending library; discounts on groceries—are yet another reason to use and be loyal to Amazon. REI has a low-cost one-time membership fee that gives customers many benefits like annual dividends on purchases, members-only deals, and the right to vote on the company's board of directors. As we discussed, you have to be a member to shop at a Costco warehouse. Your local gym likely has a membership program that provides perks, from free classes to tanning beds to childcare, which makes it less likely you will work out elsewhere.

SCALE TALL WALLS

Economies of scale is another way to build tall walls. Companies like Walmart, Costco, Amazon, United Parcel Service (UPS), and Procter & Gamble all have cost and logistical advantages they can pass on to customers. For example, supply-chain management allows Walmart and Costco to build close relationships with suppliers to drive down prices or get access to unique products (by the way, those same relationships lead to better inventory management and lower costs—financial execution). If a company like Unilever or Nestle wants to get a product on a resellers' shelves, their market power, which comes from their scale, gives them an advantage.

Sometimes the financial resources and expertise needed to be successful that come with scale are so superior that they provide tall walls automatically. A prime example of this is the building of large commercial airplanes. While the aviation industry is humongous and has the competition levels to match (just think about all the airlines, suppliers, aerospace R&D, airport operations, and regulatory agencies), there are really only two major commercial airline manufacturers that command domestic and international air space: Boeing and Airbus.

Plane manufacturers have been able to construct such tall walls because of the exorbitant amount of capital it takes to build airplanes. To put it in proper perspective, let's look at the Boeing 787. The cost of the research and development for the 787 Dreamliner was $15 billion—that's what the company invested in order to design the plane, but that doesn't include the cost of parts (of which there were 2.3 million[22]), materials, labor, and maintenance. Boeing reported the total expenditure to be $32 billion and predicted that it would take ten years and a sale of 1,100 Dreamliners for them to recoup the costs and finally break even on their investment.[23]

NETWORK EFFECTS TALL WALLS

So far, we've touched on many ways to build tall walls—patents, execution walls, product design, brand, marketing programs, and economies of scale. The next one is especially relevant in today's climate since it's about network effects, which became more of "a thing" when we built this little layer of technology for communication around our planet that we call the internet.

A network effect occurs when increasing the number of people who use a product or service improves the product or service; increases in usage lead to direct increases in value. The internet itself is a network effect. As more and more people used it, companies created more and more websites and content, which attracted even more people, which attracted even more websites and content, which attracted even more people. Network effects are a strong tall wall option for tech companies (specifically for software and web businesses), and many tech companies use this strategy; in fact, one study found that network effects account for 70 percent of the value creation in tech.[24]

There are many types of network effects that can help you build tall walls. One compelling article I read recently outlined 13 different types and counting.[25] But when it comes to building tall walls and building a winning strategy, I think there are four types of network effects that are most relevant:

- Platform network effects
- Social network effects
- Data and marketplace network effects
- Market network effects

Platform network effects

The first are platform network effects. The success of Windows led to Windows apps, which led to more Windows users, which led to even more Windows apps and even more users. The success of the Xbox and the PlayStation led to the development of lots of games, which led to more Xbox and PlayStation users and more games and more users and so on. Salesforce and many other software business products are also platforms supported by third-party software products that add value to their core offerings. The Apple iPhone and iPad with iOS and Google with its Android smartphone operating system built large user bases that led to tons of smartphone apps, which led to even more users and more apps. Today, there are millions of apps available for phones and tablets, and this makes it hard for anyone else to compete because developers can't afford to build apps for a mobile operating system that doesn't already have millions of users.

In these cases, all the network effects are enhanced because these platform products and services do even more than encourage third parties to write applications—they also provide a business opportunity for companies to develop ancillary products or services that support the platform. In the case of the phone, they build cases, charging cords, and keyboards, create YouTube videos, and author books. For enterprise platforms, companies offer installation, customization, training, and maintenance. All those products are yet another reason to own an iPhone, or another popular phone like the Samsung, or choose a CRM (customer relationship management) platform like Salesforce.

Platform network effects, like many network effects, are demand driven—the more consumers demand a product, the more attractive that product is for the next potential customer. If consumer demands shift, the network effects can evaporate. That's what happened with AOL.

AOL was once a dominant service that had its own private network of content for its users. AOL was like a mini internet—it had tons of content and services like email and messaging and chat, but as the internet grew, there was no way that AOL could keep up. When faced with competition from the open web, AOL's dominance quickly faded—it went from having 34 million subscribers to giving away email accounts and software previously available only to its paying customers. The lesson? Not all businesses that create platform (or other) network effects can keep them over time, especially as technology changes, even if those effects provide walls that are more difficult for competitors to scale.

Social network effects

The emergence of the internet was a fundamental technology change that impacted not just AOL, but entire industries and business worldwide. Facebook, WhatsApp, Instagram, LinkedIn, Slack, Skype, WeChat, Twitter, and other services exhibit social network effects (though Facebook has some platform network effects elements as well), and almost all of them were created because of the web. If you want to connect, communicate, or collaborate with your friends, coworkers, or business associates, you want to use the services where they are, and as more people use those services, they attract even more users. That is the essence of a social network effect.

Facebook, free on the web and focused on connecting users and not needing to produce or curate all its content, is much more likely to have a tall wall longer than AOL did. During the early years of Facebook, Mark Zuckerberg focused on retention. He measured it by daily active users (DAU) over monthly active users (MAU), and during the first 18 months, this number for Facebook went from 52 percent to 55 percent to 57 percent. This showed that people stayed in the network, and it wasn't just a viral growth engine; people came, connected, interacted, and stayed.

Facebook had always taken a very "clustered approach" to growth. It launched at Harvard and could have easily quickly expanded to all schools, but it didn't. Zuckerberg focused on refining the product until over half of the undergraduate population had a profile.[26] He wanted to achieve an extremely high bar of engagement before expanding—a stretch goal. One of the early criticisms of Facebook was that it didn't grow fast enough, but its expansion was strategic. Until it hit a high bar for retention, it didn't continue with its rollout. (Plus, Zuckerberg wanted to make sure the technology worked. If you grow too fast, you're more likely to have problems scaling with network stability and performance.)

Back then, Facebook was merely a database of profile pages of other people at Harvard. There was no photo sharing, no News Feed, no apps, no games, no events. The interesting thing was that local bulletin-board systems (BBS), early blogging, and AOL Instant Messenger buddy lists and status updates had made ambient social awareness a some-what regular thing for young people in the late 1990s and early 2000s. Online communities—from The WELL to SixDegrees to Friendster to Myspace—predated Facebook by years. So why was Facebook the one that stuck if the idea of the social network clearly did not catch on in earlier forms and its eventual features (profiles, statuses, photos) had already been implemented by scores of other companies? What mattered about TheFacebook, as it was originally known, was how it worked, which is to say, how it made users feel and behave.

It generated a new kind of reality, one where online activity became permanently tangled with offline selves, where a relationship wasn't real unless it was posted on Facebook, where everyone was assumed to have an online presence. And once the company gained a clear leading position compared to competitors, it became much more attractive, and a winner-take-all effect set in. Direct competitors—like Myspace early on or Google+ much later—got left behind, not necessarily because those social media services were in any way technically less well developed, but rather because Facebook worked better, focused more on personal and social connections, was a lot easier to use, and was quick to adapt to what users wanted. As a result, Facebook achieved high visibility and widespread popularity and tremendous momentum. And that is what the social network effect is really all about. You want to be on Facebook because your friends are on Facebook. It is hard to leave if you want to stay connected with your friends. Facebook became the epicenter of social networking, even if no one originally had any idea how big the quake would be.

After 2004, Facebook's network eventually extended to other Boston universities, the entire Ivy League, and then all US universities. Four years after it was founded, Facebook hit 100 million users. Four years after that, 1 billion. Today, over 2 billion people use Facebook every month[27] (which is 500 million more users than the total number of personal computers in use around the globe[28]).

Yet while the emergence, growth, and dominance of Facebook is an amazing business story and a great example of social network tall walls, it is also a cautionary one. Since the 2016 election, Facebook has faced scandal after scandal involving data, privacy, misinformation and fake accounts, and hate speech. To pick just a few examples, in April 2018, Facebook revealed that Cambridge Analytica used information belonging to 87 million Facebook users without their permission to try to influence how Americans voted in the 2016 election. In June 2018, a *New York Times* investigation revealed that, for over a decade, Facebook had been sharing data with at least 60 different companies without users' explicit consent. In August 2018, Facebook announced it had banned 20 organizations and individuals in Myanmar spreading hate and misinformation about the Rohingya genocide and refugee crisis and acknowledged it had been too slow to react. In September 2018, the company discovered a breach affecting 30 million people. In November, it admitted that an executive hired a public relations firm to attack the philanthropist George Soros, and that same month, another *New York Times* investigation concluded that Facebook had not been transparent about the extensive effort by Russia to use Facebook to disrupt the 2016 election via fake accounts, misinformation, and propaganda. In May 2019, Facebook revealed it had taken down 2.2 billion fake accounts in the first quarter of that year alone.[29] In July 2019, the FTC approved a record fine of roughly $5 billion against Facebook for mishandling users' personal information.[30] In October 2019, Facebook received strong criticism because it refused to take down a transparently false video about former Vice President Joe Biden.[31]

It is likely that some of Facebook's mistakes were blunders and poor judgment, and other mistakes were just plain greed and dishonesty. The latter is an unfathomable breach of users' trust, and both are bad for business and certainly poked holes in Facebook's reputation and its tall wall; the company has opened itself up to more oversight and scrutiny from governments, press, and users. While the data is not definitive, it does appear that Facebook usage declined in 2017, 2018, and at least some of 2019.[32] But Facebook, with its over 2 billion users, is a tall wall indeed, and its 2019 financial results were strong. I can only imagine how much stronger these three years would have been without all the mishaps and scandals.

Facebook's blunders, the tragic plane crashes resulting from flaws in Boeing's 737 Max, and the scrutiny of the practices of Google, Apple, Amazon, and other major tech players adds an important dimension to the conversation of tall walls—they can be effective and game-changing as a business strategy, and yet, if they're not maintained well and with the utmost care and oversight, hubris, greed, or just an unwillingness to keep long-term strategy first can have catastrophic or extensive negative consequences.

Data and marketplace network effects

Facebook is more than just a social network effect business. It also has data network effects. Data network effects occur when the more users use your product, the more data they contribute; the more data they contribute, the more useful your product becomes. Amazon, Google, Yelp, IMDB, Rotten Tomatoes, and Waze are examples of this; although, the relationship between product usage and the amount of *useful* new data gathered is often asymmetrical. For instance, a greater number of reviews for a greater number of restaurants on Yelp makes the product more valuable. But only a small percentage of users produce the data; most people read reviews on Yelp but don't write them. The network effect comes to fruition when a data site like Yelp or Rotten Tomatoes gets enough critical mass of information that it becomes a key site or the de facto site for users to go to. Google has a different type of data network effect. The company has so much user data to help it personalize and maximize advertising revenue that it makes it difficult for others to compete.

Marketplaces can be another type of network effect that can build tall walls. Marketplaces occur where multiple buyers and sellers accumulate around a site and there are enough of them that the site becomes a central destination for the marketplace and builds a network effect and taller walls.

Some marketplaces are product-based, such as eBay or Amazon or Etsy, while others are service-based, such as Tinder, Indeed, Airbnb, Uber, Lyft, Upwork (a marketplace for skilled freelancers), and Rover (a marketplace for pet sitters and dog walkers). Craigslist is a hybrid marketplace where both services and products are for sale. Crowdfunding marketplaces like Kickstarter, Indiegogo, GoFundMe, and CrowdRise are where philanthropies or startup projects get funded.[33]

There are plenty of business-to-business marketplaces as well. Alibaba.com is the world's largest global e-commerce platform for small and medium-sized businesses around the world. Another is ThomasNet.com, once known for *The Thomas Register of American Manufacturers*, which has operated for over 120 years and transformed itself into a data, platform, and technology company that became a leading industrial marketplace. Over a half-million suppliers and over a million buyers, engineers, and other business-purchasing decision makers use ThomasNet each month.[34]

Market network effects

A newer type of network effect that builds tall walls is called a market network. Market networks tend to target more complex, higher-value services where multiple vendors need to network and work together to get things done for a client, such as remodeling a home or planning a wedding. Market networks tend to have three key components: a marketplace for transactions, a network of vendors that work with each other, and some type of workflow software that helps track the project.

HoneyBook is a client management software platform aimed at small businesses, entrepreneurs, and freelancers mostly in creative fields. A writer can build a profile and use HoneyBook's web software to send branded proposals to clients and sign contracts digitally. Additionally, the writer can network and collaborate on HoneyBook with other professionals needed for the project, like graphic designers, printers, and photographers. Together, they form a virtual team to service a client, send each other proposals, sign contracts, and get paid.

AngelList is a market network. Investors find startups to invest in, and the startup completes the fundraising paperwork through the AngelList SaaS (software as a service) workflow, and everyone in the network can share deals, hire employees, and find customers. Legal.io is a market network in the legal industry that helps company legal departments manage projects and cases via a global network of legal professionals. LiquidSpace is a market network for renting office or working space. Joist and Houzz are market networks for the home remodel and construction industry.[35]

Houzz co-founder and CEO Adi Tatarko started the home design site with her husband after their own home remodeling process went awry. In addition to finding it difficult to communicate their vision for their home, they struggled to find the right professionals for their project. They wanted a place to browse and save beautiful home photos, find the right design and construction professionals, and ultimately, connect with others who were going through the same thing (or who'd already gone through it).

The platform started in 2009 as a humble website that displayed images of home interiors and included a handful of design portfolios from local Bay Area architects. Today, it's a highly active community of homeowners, architects, designers, and constructors with 40 million monthly unique visitors who browse 2.3 million online profiles of active professionals from all over the world.[36] It's also a hub for interactive tools where users can ask questions, learn about and purchase products, and even use virtual product placement in their homes before buying. It's become the biggest residential remodeling community online, and the essence of its success stems from the mass connections its network provides.

SHORT WALLS CAN PROVIDE OPPORTUNITY

While tall walls help grow and entrench success, short walls are sometimes an opportunity. If you are looking to enter or expand to a new market, generally short walls are the way to go. Short walls are self-explanatory—they're walls that are easier to get over, even though some scaling is definitely still required, and obviously there will still be obstacles along the way. Climbing small walls has a lot to do with the competitive environment and the resources required to succeed in business, which is why it usually makes sense to enter markets without material barriers to entry.

To pick a dramatic example for effect, going head-to-head against Amazon AWS or Microsoft Azure with a cloud platform business is probably not going to end well. The capital, expertise, and startup costs required for those businesses are vast. You'd need massive, sophisticated data centers, material operations expertise, top-notch engineers, support programs for customers and developers, and so on and so forth; those barriers are prohibitive for almost any business outside of Google and a few others. That's why, strategically, it's smarter to climb short walls. In this case, that would mean looking for niches that Amazon or Microsoft don't cover or building on top of their existing products.

Similarly, climbing short walls means tackling businesses where you have access to the assets and expertise that you need. Many folks start restaurants without having proper knowledge of the business, unsure about how to procure things like financing, food sourcing, staffing, commercial leasing, and permits and licenses. Retail owners are often unprepared for the merchandising, inventory, POS systems, marketing, and pricing philosophies that are crucial to their success. People in the manufacturing or transportation sectors are hit hard with government regulations, and whether it's figuring out complicated tax codes or complying with stipulations, the red tape presents headaches for those who lack the experience and resources of their more established competitors.

In many cases, strategic openings to create network effects only become available after certain levels of success with simpler products—the idea being to initially attract users with a single-player tool and then, over time, get them to participate in a network. Think of the tool as a way to get to initial critical mass. For example, Instagram's initial hook was their cool photo filters. At the time, some other apps like Hipstamatic had filters, but you had to pay for them. Instagram also made it easy to share your photos on other networks like Facebook and Twitter. But you could also share on Instagram's network, which of course became the preferred way to use Instagram over time.

Another option is to start in a minuscule market and create localized momentum and then expand. As I discussed, Facebook got started at Harvard. They began with a tight social circle and slowly expanded to other colleges and universities over time and then opened up the network more broadly after that.

Nextdoor, the social networking service for neighborhoods, launched in 2011 as a way to connect people in their local communities—from babysitter recommendations to getting a referral for a plumber to reporting a lost dog and much, much more. What started as a small beta test in the Lorelei neighborhood of Menlo Park, California, grew to 3,500 neighborhoods by the summer of 2012, 40,000 neighborhoods, or roughly one in four American communities by the summer of 2014, and 100,000 neighborhoods by 2016. By 2019, Nextdoor was the world's largest private network for neighborhoods, used in more than 236,000 of them throughout the United States, the United Kingdom, Germany, France, Italy, the Netherlands, and more.[37]

In other words, slowly bake it till you make it.

As we've seen, there are many ways to build tall walls. They can be government regulated and time sensitive, like Pfizer's. They can come from having an iconic brand and large-scale distribution, like Spanx. They can form because of a machine-consumables business model, like Nespresso. They can be secured through loyalty or membership programs, like credit cards with their point systems or Amazon with its Prime subscription. They can be for the prestigious few who have the resources and bandwidth for massive scale, like Boeing. They can grow as tall as the demand they garner using network effects—platform network effects like Windows and Xbox and PlayStation, social network effects like Facebook, data network effects like Yelp, marketplace network effects like Craigslist (or business-to-business ones like Alibaba.com), and market network effects like HoneyBook and Houzz. In the end, a successful business demands that the different types of tall walls are considered and implemented as part of your strategy.

PART III

EXPONENTIAL EXECUTION TIPS

CHAPTER 8

Execution

When I look back at the whole Windows 95 experience—the challenge of building such a great product and all the difficult engineering tradeoffs that had to be made, the partnerships needed to pull it all together, the methodical marketing strategy for rolling out its release—I see it as one of the most phenomenal team efforts I've ever been involved in. It was a great group of people who cared about the right things, and it was rewarding, not because of what we did, but how we did it.

In the beginning, we had no idea what we were getting into. We worked 80- to 100-hour weeks for many months. All the different teams had their set objectives—make Windows 95 easy to use, make it compatible with existing hardware and software, make it a consumer phenomenon, make it change the way people think about and interact with personal computers—and then mass amounts of structure was put in place to ensure the right people, resources, and skill sets were being used. It was organized chaos at its finest.

When Brad Silverberg, the vice president in charge of Windows 95, said, "It needs to be easy enough for my mom to use it, and she doesn't use computers," enormous effort went into turning something as complex and hard to understand as MS-DOS and earlier versions of Windows into a single user experience; it was the first Microsoft operating system that was really designed with users in mind.

When we decided it needed to be compatible with all the existing hardware and software out there, David Cole, the head of Windows engineering, went down to the local Egghead Software store and bought one of everything he could find that would run on Windows 3.1. As I discussed earlier, we also ran a massive beta test to seek out bugs we needed to fix. But those are just a couple of examples of a comprehensive, deliberate, thorough, and creative process that not only created a better, more exciting product but also showed everyone that Microsoft would do what it took to get the job done without sacrificing quality.

When I came up with the Educate, Excite, Engage launch strategy, it required each team in my marketing group to develop a plan specific to their customers, whether that meant consumers, businesses, press, partners, or developers. That tailored approach was key to the effective mass release of the product. And even though the product in and of itself was more than worthy of the hype and by far the most important reason for the success of Windows 95, I like to think the execution by my team helped set the precedent that it was worthy of a major media event in the first place.

In the end, it was all about impact. Hundreds of millions of people used Windows 95, but it was bigger than that because it ushered computers into the mainstream; it brought a whole new level of work and play to all users. Microsoft had built an ecosystem and a platform that led to a whole onslaught of new applications and new hardware. It was the right product at the right time, and it was rolled out with impeccable execution.

EXECUTION IS CORE TO STRATEGY

Execution, the things you do to run the business day-to-day, may be the most underappreciated part of business success. Since strategy is your plan to compete, execution has to be central to strategy. You can't compete without it. Morris Chang, the founding chairman of Taiwan Semiconductor Manufacturing, known as the father of Taiwan's chip industry, once said, "Without strategy, execution is aimless. Without execution, strategy is useless."[1] Great execution reminds me of a perfectly synchronized, powerful rowing team. The hands are in the right place, the oars hit the water at the right time, the coxswain is perfectly steering the boat, everyone is showing amazing determination and dedication, and the team achieves perfect rhythm and astonishing velocity. Achieving execution success is just like rowing—everyone is dependent on one another. The whole must be better than the sum of the parts. And by the way, in business, as in rowing, your success is measured relative to the competition.

Strategic execution is when a component of execution is your fundamental strategic bet to gain a core competitive advantage. As we have discussed, many companies like Old Spice, Coca-Cola, and GEICO have used marketing to try to build sustainable competitive advantages. Other companies like Whirlpool have made a worldwide manufacturing prowess key to their strategy for building better appliances at a lower cost. In commodity businesses where you can't differentiate on customer value because the products are the same or similar, strategic execution is absolutely required.

But even when out-executing competitors is not the core strategic bet and execution and tactics are serving the strategy a company is making, execution is always central in the Strategy First model. If we look back at the Strategy = E × mc² formula, it shows the centrality of execution—it doesn't matter if you have a distinctive, compelling customer value as a part of your strategy if you can't deliver on it. Your market potential doesn't matter if you can't produce the right financial results. The right competitive advantages won't give you an edge if they're not executed appropriately. And, to top it off, it is essential to remember that strategy success is enhanced when a business is running on all cylinders—not just excelling with your core strategic bets but also extending your competitive advantages by outperforming the competition in as many areas of running a business as possible.

In Albert Einstein's equation for the theory of special relativity ($E = mc^2$), the E represents units of energy, m represents units of mass, and c^2 is the speed of light squared. The theory expresses that mass and energy are the same physical entity and can be changed into each other; the equation breaks that down by showing that, where kinetic energy is concerned, atomic power works by putting m in motion, which effectively increases the output of energy exponentially. This is the same effect achieved by having a successful strategy.

You get out what you put in. Customer value, market potential, and execution are one and the same with strategy. When each of those elements is put in motion, the output increases; each component reaches a higher level, and the strategy is elevated.

So that begs the question, how do you execute well on running a business?

DETERMINE YOUR STRATEGIC BET AND TOP-LEVEL GOALS

Like everything else in the Strategy First model, it requires planning your attack and attacking your plan, which all starts with building an execution plan. That process starts with two key thrusts: deciding on your key strategic bet(s) and setting your top-level business goals.

These two core pillars play off one another. Sometimes, with a startup for example, the key strategic bet comes first and is usually an idea on how to address a customer need. Take Airbnb. The founders had just moved to San Francisco and were having trouble paying their rent. They noticed that a well-attended industrial design conference was in town and that all hotel rooms in the city were booked. They had the idea to earn some extra cash by offering visitors a place to sleep and breakfast in the morning, so they bought a few airbeds and quickly put up a site called "Air Bed and Breakfast." The idea succeeded, and the first official Airbnb guests were a 30-year-old Indian man, a 35-year-old woman from Boston, and a 45-year-old father of four from Utah who all slept on the founders' floor.[2]

An idea like that should be followed by a set of business goals. In small startups, that usually just means scrambling to stay alive at first, but over time, business goals become about customers or markets that you want to reach, profit and revenue goals, market share goals, and so on. But sometimes, the process works in reverse, wherein a company has a set of business goals it wants to achieve and then determines what its key strategic bet or bets will be to achieve success.

When I was asked to lead MSN in 1999, the service was floundering. After my leadership team and I spent some time evaluating the situation and looking at our business goals to achieve traffic leadership, stem our financial losses, and fix the terrible morale in the MSN division, I developed our strategy around two pillars: further promote our popular communication properties Hotmail (Hotmail is now called outlook.com) and MSN Messenger to drive traffic and user growth, and persuade that larger customer base to use the services we could make money on—search and shopping. The entire division pivoted to focus on this strategy and these priorities. We were able to turn MSN around from an unsuccessful internet service to the worldwide traffic and search leader. Search traffic, revenue, and internal team morale all more than doubled. Unfortunately, in early 2002 after I left Microsoft, priorities, goals, and leadership changed and the gains MSN and the group had made were lost.

DEVELOP A SET OF PRINCIPLES

Once the business goals and the strategic bet are clear, businesses should develop a set of principles to represent what they stand for and how they'll work. When Uber was exposed for having a toxic culture of harassment, discrimination, and bullying, as well as employing questionable business practices, it brought in a new CEO, Dara Khosrowshahi, who announced the ride-sharing company had adopted eight new "cultural norms," and he posted about them on LinkedIn:

1. We build globally, we live locally.

2. We are customer obsessed.

3. We celebrate differences.

4. We do the right thing. Period.

5. We act like owners.

6. We persevere.

7. We value ideas over hierarchy.

8. We make big bold bets.

Khosrowshahi felt strongly that Uber's culture needed to be rewritten from the bottom up, so instead of penning those new values in a closed room, he asked the employees for their ideas. More than 1,200 of them sent in submissions, which were voted on more than 22,000 times. Input was also collected from more than 20 focus groups consisting of representatives from their Employee Resource Group and international offices.[3]

Those eight principles compelled the priorities that Uber subsequently set: the scaling of global operations, earning customers' trust, ensuring people from diverse backgrounds feel welcome, focusing on action and accountability, staying resilient, seeking out ideas from both inside and outside the company, and rising after failure so they can make the next bet. That's exactly how a company's principles and values can and should work—they help establish what you need to do so you can get where you want to go.

MAKE PRIORITIES CLEAR

If principles are the rules of the road, priorities are the specific highways that lead to your final destination. Whenever you run a business, you are implementing countless tasks, many concurrently. But, not surprisingly, some of those tasks are more important to success than others, and your priorities should be the ones that are fundamental and critical to that success. My friend Robbie Bach, longtime head of Xbox and author of *Xbox Revisited*, likes to say that you get no more than five priorities. After all, if your list is too long, you aren't making the important determination of what key factors are most critical to your success.

With the iPhone, Steve Jobs had to get the product design and user experience right or the whole success of the iPhone would be in jeopardy. When I led the turnaround of MSN, the core services we were building our strategy around had to be done well. Also, we had to transform the morale of the group (before I was asked to lead MSN, the annual employee survey placed the MSN group morale dead last in the company), or we wouldn't have the talent and motivated team members necessary to succeed.

Netflix has built a streaming service juggernaut by providing its users tons of incredible content, but CEO Reed Hastings realized that much of that content was owned by other media companies that would eventually stop licensing that content to Netflix because they would eventually start their own streaming services. So Hastings and his team began developing their own shows and movies. That bet is becoming more and more important and is a clear priority for Netflix—more than half of Netflix's 50 most popular shows, from media companies like Disney (and Marvel, owned by Disney), NBC Universal, and Warner will likely no longer be licensed to and available on Netflix because those media companies are launching their own streaming services.[4]

ACT

Once you've established your business goals, your strategic bet, your principles, and your priorities, the next step is to ACT. And yes, ACT means to get going and start executing, but it also stands for align, communicate/curate, and track.

Align

To align is to make sure you have the right resources and skills you need to succeed. First, you should audit the skill set of your team. Do you have the experience and skills present among your staff and the monetary resources needed to successfully achieve your goals, your bet(s), and your priorities? If not, can you hire people with the skills you need and acquire or develop other necessary resources? If you can't, then that is the moment to reassess whether you've chosen the right strategy.

Similarly, if the goals and strategy you've chosen are far afield from your core DNA, what you and your business are good at, then it might also be time to reflect on whether you have the right strategy for your firm. To pick a few dramatic examples, you might not realize that Life-Savers once had a soda, Hooters had an airline, Evian had a water bra, Colgate had Kitchen Entrees (frozen dinners), and Bic had disposable underwear. Not surprisingly, all of these failed for many reasons, but chief among them was that none of these companies had experience in the businesses they were entering. If they'd had the relevant experience, they would have known that all these ideas were terrible in the first place.

Second, you should ensure there is clear accountability for achieving your goals and priorities. In my experience running large businesses, I've found that execution fails most often when there isn't a single person and team clearly responsible for your key priorities. And similarly, assuming they have the right skill set, it is wise to hold your best people accountable for your key priorities. It is also critical that the key priorities are properly funded. Do those teams have the right number of people in their group? Do they have an ample budget? If you are GEICO betting on marketing and building a brand to win with car insurance, you surely don't want to underfund marketing.

Finally, align means taking the high-level bets and goals and priorities for the company and making sure those translate consistently to the team goals throughout the company. In small companies, that's not difficult, but in larger companies, teams can easily get off strategy and work on things that don't achieve the primary mission. In addition, teamwork and collaboration across groups, often difficult in large companies but essential to success, is enhanced when there is clarity and alignment of company and team goals and clear priorities. If you don't have that in large companies, lots of problems occur—fiefdoms develop, effectiveness decreases, and sometimes bureaucracy and negative company "politics" increase.

Communicate/Curate

You need to communicate and curate your strategy and culture. To achieve success, it's important to regularly communicate with your team not only what the strategy, goals, and priorities are but also what each team's role is in carrying out the strategy. Again, in smaller companies, that's not as difficult, but in larger companies, it can be more of a challenge. Now you may say that this is obvious—*of course* a company needs to communicate its strategy, goals, and priorities to its employees. Shockingly, it turns out that most companies don't.

A 2012 survey by consultant and author and William Schiemann concluded that only 14 percent of the organizations he polled reported that their employees have a good understanding of their company's strategy and direction.[5] Now even if that number is not scientific and only in the ballpark, it probably surprised you. When I took over MSN, there was no strategy, and no one understood what was going on. I communicated to the thousands of people who worked for me what process I was going to implement so we could agree on a direction, and once I settled on the new strategy with my leadership team, we rented a large convention space in town, and I presented the new strategy live on stage and answered questions. I sent frequent emails to follow up and give people progress reports, and my leaders did the same with their teams. The leadership team and I also made sure that the strategy cascaded down and reflected in the performance review goals and objectives for everyone working on MSN. The team's understanding of the strategy and what they were working to achieve was a key reason morale in the group improved so dramatically.

For strategies to be effectively implemented, they rely on the input and commitment of a wide range of individuals who need to be involved and informed about the process from its earliest stages. Communication ensures that everyone is aware of the plan, its importance, and how they might be impacted. This creates engagement, generates broad input, helps test assumptions, and shows employees they're respected enough to be kept in the loop. If you ask any company that has ever successfully executed a strategic plan, they'd tell you that communication was imperative to their success. Employees can't execute well on a plan they don't know about. And the best part about it is there isn't just one way to implement effective communication.

Credit Karma, the San Francisco–based personal finance company acquired by Intuit Inc., the parent company of TurboTax, for $7.1 billion in 2020, has had an open-door policy since its inception in 2007. Their founder and CEO, Ken Lin, says he's always seen theirs as a mission-driven business, and it's harder for his employees to get on board if they have no access to him and instead have to accept his ideas wholesale. He also holds a monthly, town-hall meeting for employees that serves as a check-in and a back-and-forth discussion where they can ask him questions. "Credit Karma employees have quizzed me on the thinking behind office upgrades, stock options, company strategy, and expansion plans. I've even been asked about how management felt about purchasing a bartending robot."[6]

Another cool thing Lin does is bring the entire company together to share board presentations with them; he wants all employees to understand where the company is in its journey, how the business is doing, and the strategy behind it all. They rent a hotel conference room in order to fit all their employees and present the board report in full—every line item, growth chart, and product plan. Lin says a company that shares information openly and often can empower their employees to go about their jobs with confidence and know the bigger picture they're all working toward.

In some cases, CEOs have implemented quite novel approaches to company communication. At Square, the Silicon Valley–based mobile-payments company, they have a "responsible transparency" policy, which requires that when two or more people meet, one person must take notes and share them with all other interested Square employees to peruse; post-meeting, the notes are emailed to an alias and accessible to all 600 employees worldwide. Jack Dorsey, Square's co-founder and CEO (as well as the co-founder and CEO of Twitter), said he started the policy, in a way, to benefit himself because it's too difficult to keep secrets. He said eventually people will figure out what you're trying to keep from them, and it's better to just put that information out there.[7]

At the social media management company Buffer, they have no private email servers—or private emails, for that matter. Their fully transparent email system can be read by any employee at any time. For them, this ensures trust but also increases efficiency, allowing one team member to pick up on a project where the other left off without missing a beat.

But it is not enough to just communicate about strategy; it is also essential to communicate and curate the culture you want for your company. A strong, unified culture is the foundation of effective execution and successful strategy. What are the shared attitudes, values, and practices that characterize your company and that help you achieve your goals and succeed with your strategy? How do you take your core principles and shape the culture you want? What do you stand for? Customer focus? Perseverance? Risk taking? Innovation? Customer service? Adaptability? Accountability? Teamwork? Growth? Commitment to learning?

As Uber discovered, employees generally imitate the actions of their leaders. For Uber to transform its culture, just writing down a new set of principles is not enough. As the company executes its new plan, the new culture must be integral. Do employees get reviewed and rewarded for embracing the new principles and culture such as making bold bets, celebrating differences, and doing the right thing? And most importantly, are leaders practicing what they preach? If all that is not happening, then the new principles Uber is touting are meaningless, and the new culture it needs to curate will never develop.

As I mentioned earlier, it is important to be deliberate about defining your principles and the culture you want with your business. But in reality, in most young companies, the culture it not written down but emanates from the CEO and his or her team. In the early days of Microsoft, it was no different. The company culture came from Bill and the leadership team. Key elements of the company ethos were clear. The culture was dominated by self-criticality and learning, accountability, intensity, and relentlessness. Strategy was considered super important, and hiring smart people who could learn was considered more important than experience. When Microsoft did not get something right, like early versions of Windows, they kept at it, improving until things got better. Employees were never satisfied with their own efforts or the products they worked on.

For the most part, that culture and mindset worked well, but as the company grew and the industry radically changed, changing the culture was fundamental to executing the company strategy. Current Microsoft CEO Satya Nadella, hired in 2014, talked about that in his book *Hit Refresh*:[8]

> Microsoft's culture had been rigid. Each employee had to prove to everyone that he or she was the smartest person in the room. Accountability—delivering on time and hitting numbers—trumped everything. Meetings were formal. If a senior leader wanted to tap the energy and creativity of someone lower down in the organization, she or he needed to invite that person's boss, and so on. Hierarchy and pecking order had taken control, and spontaneity and creativity had suffered.

The culture change I wanted was centered on exercising a growth mindset every day in three distinct ways. First, at the core of our business must be the curiosity and desire to meet a customer's unarticulated and unmet needs with great technology. This was not abstract: We all get to practice each day. When we talk to customers, we need to listen. We need to be insatiable in our desire to learn from the outside and bring that learning into Microsoft.

Second, we are at our best when we actively seek diversity and inclusion. If we are going to serve the planet as our mission states, we need to reflect the planet. The diversity of our workforce must continue to improve, and we need to include a wide range of opinions and perspectives in our thinking and decision making. In every meeting, don't just listen—make it possible for others to speak so that everyone's ideas come through. Inclusiveness will help us become open to learning about our own biases and changing our behaviors so we can tap into the collective power of everyone in the company. As a result, our ideas will be better, our products will be better, and our customers will be better served.

Finally, we are one company, one Microsoft—not a confederation of fiefdoms. Innovation and competition don't respect our silos, so we have to learn to transcend those barriers. It's our ability to work together that makes our dreams believable and, ultimately, achievable.

Though he is the first to acknowledge "we should never be done," I think most employees support the culture reset Satya is putting in place. His "refresh" to focus on areas like customer listening and empathy, teamwork and collaboration (including with partners), and diversity are building a culture to foster innovation and growth. This culture has contributed to excellent execution as part of a winning strategy that has catapulted the company to new heights as one of the largest, and on some days *the* largest, company in the world (as measured by stock market value).

Track

T is for track, or more precisely, track to improve. No strategy and no execution plan stays the same for long. Market conditions change, competitors adjust, customers change their habits and interests. So it's necessary to track how you're doing on a regular cycle, say every six months (or less, in some cases). If market conditions are stable or changing but your strategy is solid or progressing, then you can iterate and innovate to stay ahead. But if your strategy is failing for whatever reason, it is critical to do a strategy reset and think about whether you are making the right bets.

These strategy resets, often called "pivots," happen all the time. Twitter (then named Odeo) started as a podcasting publishing platform, but in 2006 the company concluded it needed to reinvent itself because Apple had announced that iTunes would include a podcasting platform. Jack Dorsey had an idea around people giving status updates on their lives that began with a system where you could send a text message to one phone number, and the message would be broadcast to all your friends. That system eventually became Twitter.[9] Instagram began as Burbn, a check-in app that included gaming elements from *Mafia Wars*, with a photo element as well. The founders concluded that Burbn was too complex, so they took a risk and stripped all the features but one: photos. They rebuilt a version of the app with that singular focus—it was clean and simple, and the rest is history.[10] Slack, the popular cloud-based instant messaging and business collaboration platform, was originally an internal tool to connect the Canadian and US offices for Stewart Butterfield's online gaming company, Tiny Speck. When it became clear that the game would not be successful, the company realized its internal tool was the real opportunity, and Slack was born.[11]

Of course, strategy pivots and resets that come from the ongoing cycle of tracking to improve are not just for tech companies and not always as dramatic as those made by Twitter, Instagram, or Slack. In 2008, Starbucks Chairman Howard Schultz returned to the CEO role as the company was floundering. The stock had plummeted 50 percent over the previous 12 months. Schultz tells the story that he once walked into a Starbucks, and there was a table of teddy bears in the store that had nothing to do with coffee whatsoever. He asked the manager about it, and she said she was really enthused and excited because it was adding to her comps. Schultz realized this didn't make sense. The company had added too many stores too quickly and lost the essence of the coffee-house experience that was its foundation. Schultz subsequently closed poorly performing stores and refocused the strategy on its roots.

Starbucks introduced Pike Place roast to show it was serious about coffee, decided to only have whole-bean coffee delivered to its stores, required baristas to grind the beans in-store, and tossed out any coffee that had been sitting for more than 30 minutes. Starbucks also upgraded the espresso machines in all stores (and then closed down 7,100 US stores for 3.5 hours to retrain baristas on how to make the perfect espresso), reorganized and improved the supply chain, cut back on CDs and books that had started to overpower the stores, and made many other changes to get Starbucks back on strategy and growing successfully again.[12]

Another hugely successful strategy reset was Lego. From its founding in 1932 until 1998, it had never posted a loss. But by 2003, it was in big trouble. Sales were down 30 percent year-on-year, and it was $800 million in debt.[13] As Lego CEO Jorgen Vig Knudstorp put it: "We are on a burning platform, losing money with negative cash flow, and at a real risk of debt default, which could lead to a breakup of the company."[14]

Much of the blame was put on "digital natives"—that is, men and women born after 1980 who came of age in the Information Era and lacked the time and patience for Legos. Each study Lego commissioned concluded that future generations would progressively lose interest in Lego, and the generational need for instant gratification was more potent than any building block could ever hope to overcome.[15] In the face of such a prognosis, it seemed impossible for Lego to turn things around.

But then, Knudstorp rescued Lego by methodically rebuilding it, brick by brick. He analyzed all costs and dumped things it had no expertise in—the Legoland theme parks were sold, and the Lego computer games business was shut down, for example. He slashed the inventory, halving the number of individual pieces Lego produced from 13,000 to 6,500. He encouraged interaction with Lego's fans, such as through the adult Lego fan convention, Brickworld, and by launching a crowdsourcing competition where originators of winning ideas got 1 percent of their product's net sales (designs included the *Back to the*

Future DeLorean time machine, the Beatles' Yellow Submarine, and a set of female NASA scientists).

Knudstorp also made sure Lego started making popular toys again. In addition to putting a focus back on classic Lego lines like City and Space, the company created new entities: the ninja-themed Ninjago line for kids, Mindstorms kits to build programmable Lego robots for teens, and Lego Architecture for grown-up kids, including replicas of the Guggenheim, Burj Khalifa, and Robie House. Most impressive was that for a company with a customer base that in 2011 was 90 percent boys, it finally cracked the girls' market with Lego Friends, a reconfigured "mini-doll" that featured five different characters.

Finally, it leveraged existing partnerships, like with the Harry Potter, Star Wars, and Bob the Builder franchises, and, with the core business back on trek, Lego was now ready to step into new territory with a major film franchise. When the first movie, *The Lego Movie,* came out in 2014, it grossed a worldwide total of $469.1 million.[16] By 2015, the still privately owned, family-controlled Lego Group overtook Ferrari to become the world's most powerful brand.[17] In 2018, its full-year revenue was $35 billion, and it had a net profit of $7.8 billion.[18]

Tracking to improve isn't limited to product overhaul, or at least not what we think of as a standard physical product. In the late 1980s and early 1990s, the New England Patriots were a lackluster football team—they averaged fewer than seven wins a season and had never won a Super Bowl—and their stadium was in bankruptcy. After Robert Kraft purchased the team in 1994 for $172 million, he assessed the current state of the organization and determined that a new strategy around personnel, players, and their physical environment needed to be created and implemented.

He started by recruiting Bill Belichick to be the Patriots' head coach. Belichick had bounced around the league since 1975 as a defensive coordinator for the New York Giants, head coach for the Cleveland Browns, and briefly, as the head coach of the New York Jets before accepting the Patriots' offer. The same year that Belichick headed to New England, so did sixth-round draft pick Tom Brady. Today, they are widely considered to be the best head coach-QB duo of all time.[19]

Next, Kraft tackled the stadium (pun intended). With its aluminum benches that froze over during cold-weather games, inadequate plumbing, which resulted in rented portable toilets for most of the stadium's existence, and an unorganized dirt parking lot, which turned to mud during Foxborough's frequent rain,[20] he knew there could be a big payoff in upgrading the team's aging home base. After a couple of failed negotiations, Kraft privately invested 100 percent of the $325 million needed for the construction of what would become Gillette Stadium. Since it opened, every single game—preseason, regular season, and playoffs—has been sold out.

Finally, Kraft opened a 1.3 million-square-foot retail and entertainment complex next to the stadium, aptly named Patriot Place. It operates all year, not just during football season, and features an open mall, a restaurant and nightclub, a health center, a movie theater, a hotel, and a two-level interactive museum. Kraft successfully transformed the fledgling Patriots into a business powerhouse. So far, under his ownership, the franchise has won 16 AFC East division titles, made 13 appearances in the AFC Championship game, and played in nine Super Bowls with a record six wins. They are the NFL's second most profitable operation (after the Dallas Cowboys), worth an estimated $3.8 billion.[21]

The changes Schultz, Knudstrop, and Kraft made to Starbucks,

Lego, and the New England Patriots were purposeful and significant. After assessing the current state of their respective entities, they made changes to their strategies and execution plans based on shifting market conditions, competitors, and customer needs they observed; they tracked to improve.

So, once you establish your business goals, strategic bets, principles, and priorities, you then ACT—align (resources), communicate and curate (strategy and culture), and track (to improve). A lot goes into execution. But even with all those ducks in a row, and even when you pair them with things like preparation, good intentions, solid leadership, and credible products, delivering is hard. While conceptualizing what we want and plotting the course to get there can seem straightforward, when it comes to actual implementation, our strategic plans can fail for any number of reasons—but a primary reason most strategic plans never actually come to fruition is because of a failure to execute well.

If strategy starts with a fundamental bet and is a series of choices you make on where to play and how to win in order to maximize long-term value, execution is the part of strategy that produces results within the context of those choices. Some business leaders think they'd rather have great execution than superior strategies, but the truth is you can't have the first without the second. Put another way, if you execute well on a bad strategic bet, you will lose. If you execute poorly on a good bet, you will also fail. Strategy comes first, but excellent execution is required.

EPILOGUE

Keeping Strategy Central
to Your Success

I named this book *Strategy First* because if you were to rank the most important factors that contribute to the success of a business, building a winning strategy would be number one. Of course, building a winning strategy is an imperative but by no means enough. For example, as most everyone knows, leadership is critical too. Great leaders must do many things well. They must be tenacious, trustworthy, charismatic, empowering, intuitive, persuasive, influential, build great processes, build a great culture, execute well, hire great people, listen, learn, grow, adapt, and so on. The list is long, and the books on leadership are many, so I won't go into detail here. But it is critical to reinforce one thing that many leadership books don't focus on: *Successful leadership starts with strategy.* Great leadership first and foremost requires a great strategy. It is the first thing to develop when building, rebuilding, or remodeling a business. A leader who exhibits all the characteristics I mention earlier who makes the wrong bets and has an ineffective strategy won't succeed. But a leader who focuses on a winning strategy first or fixes an ineffective one quickly and does exhibit all the other key leadership qualities is likely to do very well indeed.

And that is why I wrote this book. My North Star, my goal with this book, is to make strategy understandable and approachable and help businesspeople worldwide be successful at building winning strategies. But I also want to reinforce the strategy imperative and center it at the forefront of business thinking and business leadership. After all, as I mentioned earlier in the book, I have given countless speeches on strategy over the years at companies, conferences, incubators, and business schools, and when I ask what is most important to the success of a business and a business leader, the attendees never say strategy. I hope that after attending one of my talks or after reading this book, strategy is the first thing to come to mind.

THE LEADER'S ART

But it is important to not be confused about what strategy is. I once heard a business leader say, "Strategy is results." As in, "Our strategy is to get results." From that perspective, a strategy is a lofty, self-evident statement such as "Our strategy is to pursue global expansion" or "Our strategy is to be the lowest-cost provider." Such "strategies" don't contribute much to producing results. They may motivate the troops, but even that is highly debatable. No, those blanket statements are simply goals, they're targets to hit, but they're not strategies.

Strategy is not a goal. Strategy is not a tactic. Strategy is not a vision, a process, an idea, or an inspiration. The word *strategy* comes from the Proto-Indo-European language, which existed from 4500 BC to 2500 BC, and comes from word roots that mean "to spread out" and "leader." More directly, the word *strategy* derives from the Greek word *strategos*, which means "to lead an army" or literally "the general's art." I love that concept. So if strategy is the general's art, what does a general do? He or she coordinates the whole, all of a nation's forces, with the aim of winning the war. This is the essence of business strategy—"the leader's art" is to build the plan and coordinate the whole to achieve a focused set of goals. And as we've covered, that plan to compete involves many bets, usually with one foundational, fundamental bet upon which your strategy's success or failure will be determined. If you make the wrong bet, your business will lose, but if you make the right bet and you execute well *relative to the competition*, you are on the path to success.

The relative to competition part is crucial. In his *Harvard Business Review* article titled "The Origin of Strategy," Bruce D. Henderson points out that natural competition between species has been going on for millions of years. And he reminds the reader about the biologist Georgii Gause and his principle called Gause's Law, which argues that two species competing for the same limited resources cannot coexist. Think Darwin and natural selection. This is true in business too; competitors are always jockeying to knock each other out, and you won't do well against your competition without a differentiated strategy.

But the difference in business is that business does not follow nature's generally slow-paced evolutionary principles. Leaders and their teams can use their ingenuity, smarts, logic, creativity, and so on to accelerate change and build a successful strategy, and as competitors react and market conditions and technology and external conditions change, leaders can and must evolve or reimagine their strategy to stay successful.

And that is where Einstein comes in. Okay, not really Einstein, but my riff on his most famous equation—his special theory of relativity: Strategy = $E \times mc^2$. This is the core model I introduced in chapter 1 that can help you determine the right bets to make and how to approach and build winning strategies. The E stands for execution, the m for market potential, and the c for customer value, and to purposely repeat myself, these factors matter relative to the competition.

USING THE MODEL

Whenever I give my talk, sit on boards, or advise businesspeople, they always ask how they can best use this model in their work. After all, Strategy = $E \times mc^2$ and the Strategy First Score (SFS) are not meant to be plugged into a software program that spits out a precise result.

My answer is to start with a strategy review or offsite. Generally, I suggest that one offsite meeting should take place at least once a year, and often twice a year is necessary given the rate of change in almost all businesses in today's competitive environment.

The first step of the review is a self-assessment—no sugar coating allowed. Honestly review for yourself the key questions that underlie the model. You can do this yourself, but I suggest you do it with your leadership team. What is our fundamental bet? How well are we executing in the key areas across the business? What is the market potential for the business and customers we're targeting? And finally, what is the customer value we're banking on? Then do the same assessment for your key competitors and do the comparison. Calculate SFSs like I discussed in chapter 2, if only to have a numerical gauge for the comparison. How strong or weak is your strategy relative to the competition? You can download a copy of my Strategy First Worksheet, which helps with this assessment, from my website: bradchase.net.

If you do this exercise with your leadership team, say at a strategy offsite, I highly recommend first having everyone fill out the worksheet independently. Then bring everyone together and discuss the differences in your answers. It's quite common for there to be major differences in every category, including what the fundamental bet(s) and strategy of the company really is. You'll find this process quite enlightening. It should go without saying, but the leadership team and everyone at your company should be in sync on the company's strategy.

Once you complete that process and agree on the assessment, then you can brainstorm and discuss what, if any, changes need to be made to your strategy. This is where the tools and tips and examples I discuss in the rest of the book come in handy. Can you seek technology, innovation, business model, or societal change to extend an advantage? Are there new markets, new buyers, or new ways to think about a market that can help? Warby Parker, Dollar Shave Club, Amazon Web Services (AWS), Costco, Lululemon, and the NCAA March Madness tournament were some of the examples we discussed in this section.

Can you mine a gap? Like Google, ActOne, and GEICO, can you find a key execution or customer value areas where competitors are either underperforming or not competing at all and take advantage of those opportunities? Another thing to discuss in your strategy brain-storm is whether you have or need to adapt to the tides. As we discussed in chapter 5, in every marketplace there are external factors that impact strategy—technology shifts, institutional and government policy, demographic changes, changes in the economy, environmental changes, and social trends. Kodak, Instagram, UPS, FedEx, Uber and Lyft, online food delivery, Impossible Burger, Stephen Colbert, Prosper, Indigo Agriculture, and PodShare were some of the examples I cited.

I also suggest putting aside time in your brainstorming seesion to discuss the final two tips I outline in this book. How can you expand your universe, like Apple or ESPN or YETI or the Piston Group did? Can you build taller walls by using some of the ideas we discussed in chapter 7, such as patent, execution, product, brand, marketing program, scale, or network effect tall walls?

Once you go through that process, you are only part of the way there because even when everyone agrees on the strategy for your company or business, you then have to execute well. We went over a checklist of sorts for ensuring, implementing, and maintaining effective execution: set primary goals, establish governing principles, determine your top priorities, and ACT—align (resources), communicate and curate (strategy and culture), track (to improve). I have another worksheet on my website that helps make sure your company stays focused on executing your top priorities well.

Tracking, adjusting, and remaking your strategy is often underap-preciated. Going back to the Henderson comparison between natural competition and business competition, it is important to think about strategy as living, evolving, and changing. Microsoft was a very different company when I left in 2002 than it was when I started there in 1987, and today it's even more different.

Along its journey, Microsoft has made many fundamental bets and been successful at a great number of them. Most recently, for example, current CEO Satya Nadella has successfully expanded the company bet on cloud computing, "AI" (artificial intelligence) and mobile, and as I mentioned earlier, remade the company culture to achieve the innovation and growth the company needs. Microsoft has made its share of strategic mistakes as well. Earlier in the book, I discussed the missteps the company made in the mobile space, just to pick one of many examples. The lesson? You should expect sometimes to make the wrong bet and make strategy mistakes; no person or company makes the right bets and builds the right strategies all the time. What is key is to recognize when your strategy needs changing and make the necessary adjustments. There is often a fine line between conviction that your strategy is sound and hubris that your strategy is sound. Avoid the hubris trap, stay open-minded, and make sure you have a solid process that forces you to thoughtfully track and improve or remake your strategy when you need to.

As I have mentioned multiple times in this book, another underappreciated key component of strategy is the importance of not only executing well on your fundamental bet and your top priorities, but also excelling in as many additional areas as possible. Apple first and foremost has built a wonderful, easy-to-use experience with the iPhone and the software and hardware products—like the AppStore, Apple Music, AirPods, FaceTime—that go along with it. That really is their fundamental bet on how they will out-compete other smartphone makers. That has been and should be their priority and focus. But that is not all they do. They focus on all the other details, from the quality of the screen to the processor in the phone to the experience when you visit an Apple Store. If you go back to Strategy = $E \times mc^2$ and think about the numerical representation of strategy it represents, your job is to get the E and the m and the c as high as possible. The higher you go, the higher your SFS, which means the more you will differentiate and increase your odds of success versus competitors.

Like everything else in life, a good strategy is helped by a little luck along the way too. Microsoft was fortunate that Digital Research didn't seize the opportunity to work with IBM. Apple was lucky that Steve Jobs had dinner with someone he didn't like who was boasting so much about tablet computing. Jobs decided he was going to do better—a bet that, as I described earlier, led to both the iPhone and the iPad. My great-uncle used to say, "It is better to be lucky than good." I would say it is best to be both. Or you can take the view of the Roman philosopher Seneca, who once said, "Luck is what happens when preparation meets opportunity."

One question I often get is, "What can I do if I'm not the leader or part of the leadership team developing our strategy, our fundamental bet?" First, know what the high-level company strategy is in the first place so you can execute consistently with it. The marketing team at GEICO may not have decided to bet the company on the brand-building and innovative ads they created to support that strategy, but they executed on it and had to make their own bets on the campaigns and slogans they would run. I did not make the original bet on GUI and Windows at Microsoft, Bill Gates did, but as I discussed in chapter 1, I built the E (educate, excite, engage) marketing strategy for the Windows 95 team that in and of itself was a series of bets on how best to market the product. Then each leader of my team did the same thing for the customer group they were in charge of marketing to. So while I didn't conceive the company strategy, I built the marketing strategy that was consistent with the company strategy and drove the marketing tactics we delivered on in the Windows 95 marketing plan. A company strategy cascades down the organization to smaller strategies and tactical execution. If you are not involved in the fundamental bet and company strategy, find your spot in the waterfall as the strategy cascades down through the organization.

Still another question I get asked about my model is how it works outside of the for-profit space. Can Strategy = $E \times mc^2$ help a candidate plan his or her election strategy or a nonprofit develop its business strategy? I'll talk about political strategy first. Let's assume that market potential in the political arena is the potential number of votes for a candidate in an election. In campaigns, voters can be divided into various buckets, such as people who never vote, people who sometimes vote, people who vote Democratic, people who vote Republican, and people, often independents, who go back and forth. So based on the candidate and their party affiliation, they have a voter or market potential in whatever local, state, or national election they're in. In addition, most candidates are making fundamental bets on what they stand for, how they connect with voters, and what they think will sway voters. I'll call those things customer value. Then they have to execute well—get their message out, build policies, do well in debates, get out the vote, build relationships with influentials, raise money, raise more money, and so on and so on. And importantly, success in both customer value and execution matter relative to the competition. We might debate whether we still square the c, but conceptually the strategy model seems to work pretty well for political campaigns.

For example, if you're a Democratic candidate in an election where most of the voters in your district are Republican, then you are going to have to dramatically outperform the candidate you are up against in customer value and execution in order to prevail. That's how Doug Jones won the 2017 special senate election in Alabama, a very heavy Republican state. It was all relative, of course, because his opponent, Roy Moore, was alleged to have sexually assaulted and accused of sexual misconduct by several women, including some who were minors. Jones was a well-respected attorney and former prosecutor, so his customer value and the execution of his campaign was enough to overcome the higher voter or market potential that Moore had started with.

The nonprofit space is a bit trickier. Certainly every nonprofit makes bets, and usually there is a fundamental bet on what problem the nonprofit is tackling, such as social justice, helping kids, education, climate change, providing food or shelter to people who need it, democratic reforms, global health, the arts, and so on. And certainly execution is important to all nonprofits as well. But there are multiple customers for most nonprofits. There are the users, the choosers, and people who pay the dues, a phrase coined by Michael Free, an instructor in the Department of Global Health at the University of Washington. The users are the people the nonprofits are trying to help, but sometimes there are choosers who control access to the users.

For example, governments often control access to their citizens impacted by a natural disaster. When choosers exist, they too are customers. Finally, there are the donors, the people who pay the dues. Donors have different needs and issues, and so nonprofits need to consider how they provide value to them as well. So if you want to use the model to help build your nonprofit strategy, you probably have to adjust it to account for the value proposition you have for the different customers involved.

Ultimately though, even if the model needs a touch of tweaking for the nonprofit space, or to be used for things like elections, the core point remains the same: Strategy First.

My hope is that you now have a clear and comprehensive understanding of why strategy is the business success imperative and why winning strategies help businesses win big. I hope that hearing the stories of businesses that deployed successful strategies, as well as learning about ones whose flawed strategies ultimately failed, gave you insight into the absolute necessity of a well-crafted strategy and how an ill-prepared, underdeveloped one will lead to the failure of your business endeavors. I hope the formula, scoring system, key elements, and tips we covered will guide you as you make your way through inevitable market shifts, temperamental economies, fervent competitors, and countless external factors that will threaten your progress. But mostly, I hope you're going to close this book feeling equal parts challenged, inspired, and compelled to make big bets of your own, big bets that are backed up by winning strategies.

Acknowledgments

When I started doing strategy talks four years ago, I had several goals. One of them was to spread the strategy gospel broadly. I felt like strategy had lost its luster, even though no business is successful without a winning strategy. I also wanted to share a compelling, simple, memorable, and useful model for how to think about and build successful strategies that would help a wide range of business leaders and aspiring business leaders.

But when attendees of my talk, family, and friends suggested that I adapt the talk into a book, I was hesitant. I have done boatloads of public speaking but had never written a book. So first I chatted with folks who had some experience. My friend Robbie Bach, longtime Xbox leader and author of *Xbox Revisited*, was very generous with his advice. I also got useful tips from a longtime Microsoft colleague, Greg Shaw. He is the co-author of *Hit Refresh* by Satya Nadella. Greg is a fountain of knowledge about the publishing industry. Julie Weed, writer for the *New York Times* and *Forbes*, also shared some lessons learned from writing her book *All I Really Need to Know in Business I Learned at Microsoft: Insider Strategies to Help You Succeed.*

My friend Mike Eck thought my strategy ideas would be valuable to a lot of businesspeople and pushed me to get going. He had me talk to his son, Connor, who works in the publishing industry. Connor also gave me some helpful suggestions. Another friend, Jim Horgdal, provided encouragement and ideas and was a sounding board from the earliest days of my Strategy First talk and book development.

I got referred to three people who had written successful books and were generous enough to talk to me, even though we had never met: Amy Jo Martin, Nell Scovell, and Erik Wahl. I appreciate their time and advice.

Brent Cole and Krista Morgan get thank-yous for their help with the writing process. Erika Shaffer referred me to some experts to help me with marketing the book.

Inspired by all the photos of Albert Einstein working at a chalkboard, Alicia Thornber conceived the superb and lauded PowerPoint chalkboard designs that appear in my talk and the book. Teresa Muniz crafted the brilliant cover, page design, and overall book design for *Strategy First.* I also appreciate how Alicia and Teresa collaborated to make the book and presentation designs harmonious.

Teresa is part of the stellar team at Greenleaf Book Group, who have been pivotal in every facet of the publishing process. Daniel Pederson and Jen Glynn navigated the ship as project managers. Lindsey Clark did a terrific job as lead editor. Steven Elizalde, the Greenleaf sales and distribution leader, was patient with all of my questions and even more insightful in answering them. Also, thanks to Justin Branch, who ushered me into Greenleaf in the first place.

A few business leaders did me the favor of reviewing their company story. Thanks to Jim Sinegal for his help with the Costco story, Bill Roberts with GEICO, and Andy Jassy and Leah Bibbo at Amazon.

I also appreciate the help from Laurie Raisys, owner of our fantastic local book store, Island Books. Laurie gave me some good ideas and suggestions for the book cover design and for selling books via independent bookstores.

Thanks to John Ludwig, Amy Shenkan, and Robbie Bach for reading parts of the draft manuscripts. Special thanks to my former longtime boss and mentor, Brad Silverberg, who read the entire manuscript and provided very valuable feedback.

I'd also like to acknowledge my former colleagues and friends from Microsoft. So many of them were pivotal to my growth and success as a business leader. And a second thanks to those who helped with the book. Gratitude also to Satya Nadella for writing the foreword and to Greg Shaw and Frank Shaw (no relation) for helping make the foreword possible.

I'd like to give special recognition to my mom and my brother. And thank you to my friends and extended family, who are so important to me and who have been so supportive of this book project. In particular, a shout-out to all three of my adult sons, who read manuscripts and provided valuable feedback, encouragement, and support. Thank you Ben, Sam, and David. Finally, a very special thanks to my wife, Judy, who read multiple drafts and provided tons of clever ideas, thoughtful input, and additional encouragement. If the business success imperative is strategy, then my family is the life success imperative. The family plan is the most important plan of all. I'd like to dedicate this book, and my love and thanks, to them.

It takes a village.

Notes

INTRODUCTION

1. "The Television Program Transcripts: Part II," PBS, https://www.pbs.org/nerds/part2.html.

2. Michael J. Miller, "The Rise of DOS: How Microsoft Got the IBM PC OS Contract," PC Mag.com, August 10, 2011, https://forwardthinking.pcmag.com/software/286148-the-rise-of-dos-how-microsoft-got-the-ibm-pc-os-contract.

3. "The Television Program Transcripts: Part II," PBS, https://www.pbs.org/nerds/part2.html.

CHAPTER 1

1. Megumi Fujikawa, "Marie Kondo Says You Can Have More Than 30 Books, Just Wake Them Up First," updated February 1, 2019, *The Wall Street Journal*, https://www.wsj.com/articles/marie-kondo-says-you-can-have-more-than-30-books-just-wake-them-up-first-11549008700.

2. Christoph Dernbach, "How Windows 95 Started a Craze," August 21, 2015, https://www.iol.co.za/business-report/companies/how-windows-95-started-a-craze-1903736.

3. Tomás Quiñonez-Riegos, "#innovator2watch: Yscaira Jimenez," BIF Speak, June 13, 2016, https://medium.com/bif-speak/innovator2watch-yscaira-jimenez-5bf5cad57aa7.

4. David Rock and Heidi Grant, "Why Diverse Teams Are Smarter," *Harvard Business Review*, November 4, 2016, https://hbr.org/2016/11/why-diverse-teams-are-smarter.

5. "The Top 20 Reasons Startups Fail," CBInsights, February 2, 2018, https://www.cbinsights.com/research/startup-failure-reasons-top/.

6. Matthew Panzarino, "Facebook Buying WhatsApp for $19B, Will Keep the Messaging Service Independent," TechCrunch, February 19, 2014, https://techcrunch.com/2014/02/19/facebook-buying-whatsapp-for-16b-in-cash-and-stock-plus-3b-in-rsus/.

7. Chinmay Rautmare, "WhatsApp User Base Crosses 2 Bln Mark, Second Only to Facebook," ed. Shinjini Ganguli, *Reuters*, February 12, 2020, https://www.reuters.com/article/whatsapp-users-idUSL4N2AC3W1.

8. Sarah Harris, "The Creative Force behind J. Crew," *The Guardian*, April 28, 2012, https://www.theguardian.com/fashion/2012/apr/29/j-crew-fashion-jenna-lyons.

9. United States Securities and Exchange Commission, Form 8-K, J. Crew Group, Inc., http://investors.jcrew.com/static-files/e36c95dc-94d6-4871-b45b-2aa1927d8b68.

10. Moody's Investors Service, "Rating Action: Moody's Downgrades J. Crew's CFR to B3 from B2, Outlook Stable," December 5, 2014, https://www.moodys.com/research/Moodys-downgrades-J-Crews-CFR-to-B3-from-B2-outlook--PR_314478.

11. Suzanne Kapner, "J.Crew Hires Former Victoria's Secret Executive as CEO," *The Wall Street Journal*, January 28, 2020, https://www.wsj.com/articles/j-crew-hires-former-victorias-secret-executive-as-ceo-11580245080?mod=djemalertNEWS.

12. Dan Bigman, "How General Motors Was Really Saved: The Untold True Story of the Most Important Bankruptcy in US

History," *Forbes*, November 18, 2013, https://www.forbes.com/sites/danbigman/2013/10/30/how-general-motors-was-really-saved-the-untold-true-story-of-the-most-important-bankruptcy-in-u-s-history/#22911f257eea.

13. James R. Healey, "Government Sells Last of Its GM Shares," *USA Today*, updated December 10, 2013, https://www.usatoday.com/story/money/cars/2013/12/09/government-treasury-gm-general-motors-tarp-bailout-exit-sale/3925515/.

14. "The Biggest Business Comebacks of the Past 20 Years," *Fast Company*, March 17, 2015, https://www.fastcompany.com/3042431/the-biggest-business-comebacks-of-the-past-20-years.

15. David Goldman, "GM Is Reinventing Itself. It's Cutting 15% of Its Salaried Workers and Shutting 5 Plants in North America," CNN Business, November 26, 2018, https://www.cnn.com/2018/11/26/business/gm-oshawa-plant/index.html.

CHAPTER 2

1. "CHM Live: Scott Forstall and Original iPhone Innovators," June 20, 2017, https://www.facebook.com/computerhistory/videos/10155442557865816/; Matt Weinberger, "The iPhone Originally Happened because Steve Jobs Hated a Guy Who Worked at Microsoft," *Business Insider,* June 21, 2017, https://www.businessinsider.com/steve-jobs-apple-iphone-hated-microsoft-2017-6.

2. "64 Million Smart Phones Shipped Worldwide in 2006," Canalys, February 12, 2007, https://www.canalys.com/newsroom/64-million-smart-phones-shipped-worldwide-2006.

3. John Mather, "iMania," *Ryerson Review of Journalism*, February 19, 2007, https://web.archive.org/web/20070303032701/http://www.rrj.ca/online/658/.

4. Arne Holst, "Global Market Share Held by Leading Smartphone Vendors from 4th Quarter 2009 to 3rd Quarter 2019," Statista, updated August 2, 2019, https://www.statista.com/statistics/271496/global-market-share-held-by-smartphone-vendors-since-4th-quarter-2009/.

5. Panos Mourdoukoutas, "Samsung Beats Apple in the Global Smartphone Market as Chinese Brands Close In," *Forbes*, September 13, 2018, https://www.forbes.com/sites/panosmourdoukoutas/2018/09/13/samsung-beats-apple-in-the-global-smartphone-market-as-chinese-brands-close-in/#7187d8ab697d; Newsroom press release, "Gartner Says Global Smartphone Sales Continued to Decline in Second Quarter of 2019," Gartner, August 27, 2019, https://www.gartner.com/en/newsroom/press-releases/2019-08-27-gartner-says-global-smartphone-sales-continued-to-dec; "Smartphone Market Share," IDC, updated June 18, 2019, https://www.idc.com/promo/smartphone-market-share/vendor.

6. "Smartphone Market Share," IDC, Updated June 18, 2019, https://www.idc.com/promo/smartphone-market-share/vendor.

7. Kevin Roos, "Apple's Biggest Problem? My Mom," *The New York Times*, January 5, 2019, https://www.nytimes.com/2019/01/05/technology/apple-iphone-replacement-mom.html.

8. Brian X. Chen, "iPhone 11 and 11 Pro Review: Thinking Differently in the Golden Age of Smartphones," *The New York Times*, updated September 19, 2019, https://www.nytimes.com/2019/09/17/technology/personaltech/iphone-11-review.html.

9. Jack Nicas and Keith Collins, "How Apple's Apps Topped Rivals in the App Store It Controls," *The New York Times*, September 9, 2019, https://www.nytimes.com/interactive/2019/09/09/technology/apple-app-store-competition.html?action=click&module=Top%20Stories&pgtype=Homepage.

10. Ben Ambridge, "The Coca-Cola Wars: Can Anybody Really Tell the Difference?" Jstor Daily, April 19, 2015, https://daily.jstor.org/the-coca-cola-wars-can-anybody-really-tell-the-difference/.

11. Samuel M. McClure, Jian Li, Damon Tomlin, Kim S. Cypert, Latané M. Montague, and P. Read Montague, "Neural Correlates of Behavioral Preference for Culturally Familiar Drinks," *Neuron*, vol. 44, 379–387, October 14, 2004.

12. Ethan Wolff-Mann, "Why Dos Equis' 'Most Interesting Man' Ad Campaign Was So Successful," *Money*,

March 9, 2016, http://money.com/money/4252403/
success-most-interesting-man-in-the-world-ad/.

13. Hadley Malcolm, "Dos Equis Retiring Its 'Most
    Interesting Man in the World,'" *USA Today*, March 9,
    2016, https://www.usatoday.com/story/money/2016/03/09/
    dos-equis-most-interesting-man-in-the-world-retiring/81432356/.

14. The GCBC Analysis, "US—Large Luxury Car Sales Figures,"
    Goodcarbadcar Auto Sales Data & Stats, http://www.goodcarbadcar.
    net/us-large-luxury-car-sales-figures/.

15. The GCBC Analysis, "US—Midsize Luxury Car Sales Figures,"
    Goodcarbadcar Auto Sales Data & Stats, http://www.goodcarbadcar.
    net/us-midsize-luxury-car-sales-figures/.

16. Zachary Shahan, "Best Car in USA, Tesla Model 3, Is 13th Best
    Selling Car in 1st Quarter—What Does That Mean?" Clean
    Technica, April 4, 2019, https://cleantechnica.com/2019/04/04/
    best-car-in-usa-tesla-model-3-is-13-best-selling-car-in-1st-quarter/.

17. Sean O'Kane, "Tesla Posts Back-to-Back Profits
    for the First Time," *The Verge*, January 30, 2019,
    https://www.theverge.com/2019/1/30/18203886/
    tesla-earnings-q1-revenue-profit-record-model-3.

CHAPTER 3

1. Bernard Marr, "The Fascinating Ways Warby Parker Uses Artificial
   Intelligence and AR to Change Retail," *Forbes*, April 18, 2019,
   https://www.forbes.com/sites/bernardmarr/2019/04/18/the-
   fascinating-ways-warby-parker-uses-artificial-intelligence-and-ar-
   to-change-retail/#61b852584b2e.

2. Jaclyn Trop, "How Dollar Shave Club's Founder Built a $1 Billion
   Company That Changed the Industry," *Entrepreneur*, March 28,
   2017, https://www.entrepreneur.com/article/290539.

3. Dan Primack, "Unilever Buys Dollar Shave Club for $1 Billion,"
   Fortune, July 19, 2016, https://www.entrepreneur.com/article/290539.

4. Michael J. de la Merced, "Shaving Startup Harry's Will Be Sold to Owner of Schick for 1.37 Billion," *The New York Times*, May 9, 2019, https://www.nytimes.com/2019/05/09/business/dealbook/harrys-edgewell-acquisition.html.

5. "Sustainability Report 2018," Warby Parker, https://www.warbyparker.com/assets/img/sustainability/report-2018.pdf.

6. Ron Miller, "How AWS Came to Be," TechCrunch, July 2, 2016, https://techcrunch.com/2016/07/02/andy-jassys-brief-history-of-the-genesis-of-aws/.

7. "Gartner Says Worldwide IaaS Public Cloud Services Market Grew 31.3% in 2018," Gartner, press release, July 29, 2019, https://www.gartner.com/en/newsroom/press-releases/2019-07-29-gartner-says-worldwide-iaas-public-cloud-services-market-grew-31point3-percent-in-2018.

8. Ron Miller, "AWS Revenue Growth Slips a Bit, but Remains Amazon's Golden Goose," TechCrunch, July 25, 2019, https://techcrunch.com/2019/07/25/aws-revenue-growth-slips-a-bit-but-remains-amazons-golden-goose/.

9. "PriceCostco, Inc. History," Funding Universe, http://www.fundinguniverse.com/company-histories/pricecostco-inc-history/.

10. Susanna Kim, "Companies That Give Health Care to Part-Time Employees," ABC News, October 7, 2014, https://abcnews.go.com/Business/companies-give-health-care-part-time-employees/story?id=26024806.

11. Steve Greenhouse, "How Costco Became the Anti–Wal-Mart," *The New York Times*, July 17, 2005, https://www.nytimes.com/2005/07/17/business/yourmoney/how-costco-became-the-antiwalmart.html.

12. Carl Quintanilla, "The Costco Craze: Inside the Warehouse Giant," CNBC, April 9, 2012, https://www.cnbc.com/the-costco-craze-inside-the-warehouse-giant/.

13. David Portalatin, "New Year, New Realities," npd.com, January 5, 2018, https://www.npd.com/wps/portal/npd/us/blog/2018/new-year-new-realities/.

14. Jarrod Davis, "Walmart Launches 2000th Online Grocery Pickup," Retail Details (blog), https://blog.8thandwalton.com/2018/09/walmart-2000th-ogp/.

15. "Online Food Delivery," Statista, https://www.statista.com/outlook/374/100/online-food-delivery/worldwide#market-users.

16. "Online Food Delivery," Statista, https://www.statista.com/outlook/374/109/online-food-delivery/united-states.

17. "Alexa, What's for Dinner Tonight," Morgan Stanley, https://www.morganstanley.com/ideas/online-food-delivery-market-expands.

18. Press Release, "Americans Will Wager $8.5 Billion on March Madness," American Gambling Association, March 18, 2019, https://www.americangaming.org/new/americans-will-wager-8-5-billion-on-march-madness/.

19. John S. Kiernan, "2019 March Madness Stats & Facts," WalletHub, March 13, 2019, https://wallethub.com/blog/march-madness-statistics/11016/.

20. "Employers Brace for March Madness," Challenger, Gray, & Christmas, Inc., 2016 March Madness Report, http://www.challengergray.com/press/press-releases/employers-brace-march-madness.

21. "2018 Tournament Viewership Attendance Numbers," April 13, 2018, "https://www.ncaa.com/news/basketball-men/article/2018-04-13/2018-ncaa-tournament-and-final-four-viewership-attendance.

22. Jason Notte, "How March Madness Stacks Up Money-Wise Against Other Sporting Events," The Street, March 11, 2016, https://www.thestreet.com/story/13491940/1/how-march-madness-stacks-up-money-wise-against-other-sporting-events.html.

23. Robert J. Szczerba, "Bracketology 101: Picking a Perfect Bracket Is Actually Easier than You Think," *Forbes*, March 17, 2015, https://www.forbes.com/sites/robertszczerba/2015/03/17/bracketology-101-picking-a-perfect-bracket-is-actually-easier-than-you-think/#385c2b52abda.

24. "Part Two: The Iconic Red Envelope," March 29, 2018, https://youtu.be/IaLF4TszLOs.

25. Marc Randolph, "He 'Was Struggling Not to Laugh': Inside Netflix's Crazy, Doomed Meeting with Blockbuster," *Vanity Fair*, September 17, 2019, https://www.vanityfair.com/news/2019/09/netflixs-crazy-doomed-meeting-with-blockbuster?utm_source=pocket-newtab.

26. Edmund Lee, "Netflix Reports a Subscriber Bump as Disney Poses a New Threat," *The New York Times*, January 21, 2020, https://www.nytimes.com/2020/01/21/business/media/netflix-q4-2019-earnings-nflx.html.

CHAPTER 4

1. Steven Levy. *In the Plex: How Google Thinks, Works, and Shapes Our Lives* (New York: Simon & Schuster, 2011): 30.

2. George Nguyen, "Now, More than 50 Percent of Google Searches End Without a Click to Other Content, Study Finds," Search Engine Land, August 14, 2019, https://searchengineland.com/now-more-50-of-google-searches-end-without-a-click-to-other-content-study-finds-320574.

3. "Worldwide Desktop Market Share of Leading Search Engines from January 2010 to July 2019," Statista, https://www.statista.com/statistics/216573/worldwide-market-share-of-search-engines/.

4. Greg Sterling, "YouTube Kicked in $15 Billion as Google Ad Revenues Topped $134 Billion in 2019," *Marketing Land*, February 3, 2020, https://marketingland.com/youtube-kicked-in-15-billion-as-google-ad-revenues-topped-134-billion-in-2019-275373.

5. Richard Nieva, "Google's Medical Data Project Spurs HHS Inquiry, Report Says," CNET, November 12, 2019, https://www.cnet.com/news/googles-medical-data-project-spurs-hhs-inquiry-report-says/.

6. Todd Haselton, "How to Find Out What Google Knows about You and Limit the Data It Collects," CNBC, December 6, 2017, https://www.cnbc.com/2017/11/20/what-does-google-know-about-me.html.

7. Nitasha Tiku, "The EU Hits Google with a Third Billion-Dollar Fine. So What?" *Wired*, March 20, 2019, https://www.wired.com/story/eu-hits-google-third-billion-dollar-fine-so-what/.

8. Courtney Connley, "How Janice Bryant Howroyd Turned a $900 Loan from Her Mom into a Billion-Dollar Business," CNBC Make It, April 20, 2018, https://www.cnbc.com/2018/04/20/janice-bryant-howroyd-used-1500-to-start-a-billion-dollar-business.html.

9. Ronald D. White, "How I Made It: Meet Janice Bryant Howroyd, the First African American Woman to Run a $1 Billion Business," *Los Angeles Times*, February 11, 2018, https://www.latimes.com/business/la-fi-himi-howroyd-20180211-htmlstory.html.

10. Federal Insurance Office, "Annual Report on the Insurance Industry," US Department of the Treasury, September 2016, https://www.treasury.gov/initiatives/fio/reports-and-notices/Documents/2016_Annual_Report.pdf.

11. Jessica McGregor and Megan Sutela, "How Advertising Spend, Underwriting Results Relate to Auto Insurers' New Business Yield: J. D. Power," *Insurance Journal*, June 19, 2017, https://www.insurancejournal.com/news/national/2017/06/19/454947.htm.

12. "Geico's Story from the Beginning," GEICO, https://www.geico.com/about/corporate/history-the-full-story/.

13. "Berkshire Hathaway Annual Meeting," 2009, https://www.scribd.com/document/14995963/Berkshire-Hathaway-Annual-Meeting.

14. Velocify, "Latest Insurance Study Reveals Strong Link between Marketing, Technology Investment, and Revenue Growth," Cision PR Newswire, May 11, 2016, https://www.prnewswire.com/news-releases/latest-insurance-study-reveals-strong-link-between-marketing-technology-investment-and-revenue-growth-300266424.html.

15. Ann-Christine Diaz, "Geico's 'Unskippable' from the Martin Agency Is *Ad Age*'s 2016 Campaign of the Year," *AdAge*, January 25, 2016, https://adage.com/article/special-report-agency-alist-2016/geico-s-unskippable-ad-age-s-2016-campaign-year/302300.

16. Erica Sweeney, "Geico Is Top Spender on YouTube While Auto Brands Slash Budgets, Analysis Finds," Marketing Dive, February 1, 2019, https://www.marketingdive.com/news/geico-is-top-spender-on-youtube-while-auto-brands-slash-budgets-analysis-f/547378/.

17. "Geico's Story from the Beginning," GEICO, https://www.geico.com/about/corporate/history-the-full-story/.

CHAPTER 5

1. "5 Major Moments in Cellphone History," CBC News, April 3, 2013, https://www.cbc.ca/news/technology/5-major-moments-in-cellphone-history-1.1407352.

2. Pascal Emmanuel Gobry, "10 Brilliant Startups That Failed Because They Were Ahead of Their Time," *Business Insider*, May 4, 2011, https://www.businessinsider.com/startup-failures-2011-5.

3. Ed Pilkington and Bobbie Johnson, "iPhone Causes Big Apple Swarm in Big Apple Storms," *The Guardian*, June 29, 2007, https://www.theguardian.com/news/2007/jun/29/usnews.apple.

4. Brand Minds, "Why Did Kodak Fail and What Can You Learn from Its Demise?," *Medium*, December 14, 2018, https://medium.com/@brand_minds/why-did-kodak-fail-and-what-can-you-learn-from-its-failure-70b92793493c.

5. David Usborne, "The Moment It All Went Wrong for Kodak," *Independent*, January 20, 2012, https://www.independent.co.uk/news/business/analysis-and-features/the-moment-it-all-went-wrong-for-kodak-6292212.html.

6. Leslie Wayne, "Kodak Agrees to Buy Sterling for $5.1 Billion," *The New York Times*, January 23, 1988, https://www.nytimes.com/1988/01/23/business/kodak-agrees-to-buy-sterling-for-5.1-billion.html; "Kodak to Sell Remaining Sterling Winthrop Unit: Drugs: SmithKline Beecham Will Buy the Consumer Health Products Business for $2.925 Billion," *Los Angeles Times*, August 30, 1994, https://www.latimes.com/archives/la-xpm-1994-08-30-fi-32940-story.html; Steve Brachmann, "The Rise and Fall of the Company That Invented Digital Cameras," IP Watchdog, November 1, 2014, https://www.ipwatchdog.com/2014/11/01/the-rise-and-fall-of-the-company-that-invented-digital-cameras/id=51953/.

7. Ernest Scheyder, "Focus on Past Glory Kept Kodak from Digital Win," Reuters, January 19, 2012, https://www.reuters.com/article/us-kodak-bankruptcy/focus-on-past-glory-kept-kodak-from-digital-win-idUSTRE80I1N020120119.

8. Jay Clarke, "Picture This: Family Photo Album Gets a Modern Update," *Providence Journal*, December 30, 2007, http://www.projo.

com/lifebeat/content/lb_photo_books_12-30-07_GH88B0A_
v6.5bc0b.html.

9. Matthew Sparkes, "Kodak: 130 Years of History," *The Telegraph*,
   January 19, 2012, https://www.telegraph.co.uk/finance/newsbysector/
   retailandconsumer/9024539/Kodak-130-years-of-history.html.

10. Felix Richter, "Digital Camera Sales Dropped 84 Percent Since
    2010," Statista, May 27, 2019, https://www.statista.com/chart/5782/
    digital-camera-shipments/.

11. "Kodak Sells OLED Unit to LG," Photonics Media,
    December 14, 2009, https://www.photonics.com/Articles/
    Kodak_Sells_OLED_Unit_to_LG/a40563.

12. Oliver Kmia, "Why Kodak Died and Fujifilm Thrived: A Tale of Two
    Film Companies," PetaPixel, October 19, 2018, https://petapixel.
    com/2018/10/19/why-kodak-died-and-fujifilm-thrived-a-tale-of-
    two-film-companies/.

13. "Fujifilm's Business Fields," Fuijifilm, https://www.fujifilm.com/
    about/profile/business_fields/.

14. "Imaging Solutions (Earnings of FY2019/3)," Fujifilm, https://
    www.fujifilmholdings.com/en/investors/ir_library/earnings_
    summary/2018/quarter4/result001/index.html.

15. "Intuit Changed TurboTax This Year, Triggering an Enormous
    Customer Uproar," *Los Angeles Times*, January 19, 2015, https://www.
    latimes.com/business/hiltzik/la-fi-mh-intuits-catastrophic-turbotax-
    20150118-column.html.

16. Shanthi Rexaline, "3 Reasons Intuit Will Continue to Dominate the
    Tax Business," Yahoo Finance, September 21, 2017, https://finance.
    yahoo.com/news/3-reasons-intuit-continue-dominate-144633656.
    html.

17. Michael Ruiz, "Is the Micro Machines Guy Still the Fastest-Talking
    Man on the Planet?," *New York Magazine*, December 9, 2016, http://
    nymag.com/speed/2016/12/is-the-micro-machines-guy-still-the-
    fastest-talking-man-on-the-planet.html.

18. Martin Murray, "The History of FedEx: How the Delivery Service
    Became a Major Player," The Balance Small Business, July 30, 2019,
    https://www.thebalancesmb.com/federal-express-fedex-2221098.

19. "About FedEx," FedEx, https://about.van.fedex.com/our-story/ history-timeline/history/.

20. "UPS from 1907–1929," UPS, https://www.ups.com/cy/en/about/ history/1907-1929.page.

21. "UPS from 1981–1990," UPS, https://www.ups.com/cy/en/about/ history/1981-1990.page.

22. "Postal Facts: Sizing It Up," USPS, https://facts.usps.com/ size-and-scope/.

23. Bill McAllister, "Continuing Decline in First-Class Mail Volume Highlights 'Strong Headwinds' Facing USPS," Linn's Stamp News, https://www.linns.com/news/us-stamps-postal-history/2017/august/ continuing-decline-first-class-mail-volume-strong-headwinds- facing-usps.html.

24. Josh Spiro, "Why Demographics Are Crucial to Your Business," *Inc.*, December 2, 2009, https://www.inc.com/news/articles/2009/12/ customer-demographics.html.

25. Karen Robinson-Jacobs, "Dallas' Pizza Patrón Chain Sold to Large Texas-Based Franchisee," *The Dallas Morning News*, January 10, 2017, https://www.dallasnews.com/business/local-companies/2017/01/10/ dallas-pizza-patron-chain-sold-to-large-texas-based-franchisee/.

26. Jack Ewing, "The Car Industry Is Under Siege," *The New York Times*, June 6, 2019, https://www.nytimes.com/2019/06/06/business/auto- industry-fiat-renault.html.

27. Pamela N. Danziger, "9 Demographic Trends Shaping Retail's Future," *Forbes*, September 6, 2018, https://www.forbes.com/sites/ pamdanziger/2018/09/06/9-demographic-trends-shaping-retails- future/#7f0181037b00.

28. QuickFacts, "San Francisco County, California," United States Census Bureau, https://www.census.gov/quickfacts/ sanfranciscocountycalifornia.

29. QuickFacts, "Los Angeles County, California," United States Census Bureau, https://www.census.gov/quickfacts/fact/table/ losangelescountycalifornia,CA/PST045218.

30. "California Housing Future: Challenges and Opportunities,"

California Department of Housing and Community Development, January 2017, http://www.hcd.ca.gov/policy-research/plans-reports/docs/California's-Housing-Future-Full-Public-Draft.pdf.

31. Crystal Chen, "Zumper National Rent Report: November 2019," Zumper, blog, October 31, 2019, https://www.zumper.com/blog/rental-price-data.

32. "Forecast 2019: The Business of Assisted Living: Growth, Construction, and Partnerships," PharMerica, June 2019, https://www.pharmerica.com/forecast-2019the-business-of-assisted-living-growth-construction-partnerships/.

33. Anthony Cilluffo and D'Vera Cohn, "6 Demographic Trends Shaping the US and the World in 2019," Pew Research Center, April 11, 2019, https://www.pewresearch.org/fact-tank/2019/04/11/6-demographic-trends-shaping-the-u-s-and-the-world-in-2019/.

34. "Our Story," Prosper, https://www.prosper.com/about.

35. "Ag and Food Sectors and the Economy," United States Department of Agriculture, https://www.ers.usda.gov/data-products/ag-and-food-statistics-charting-the-essentials/ag-and-food-sectors-and-the-economy.aspx.

36. Lori Ioannou, "This Is a $15 Trillion Opportunity for Farmers to Fight Climate Change," CNBC, June 12, 2019, https://www.cnbc.com/2019/06/11/this-is-a-15-trillion-opportunity-for-farmers-to-fight-climate-change.html.

37. NOAA, "Fast Facts: Hurricane Costs," last modified July 10, 2019, https://coast.noaa.gov/states/fast-facts/hurricane-costs.html.

38. Bill Whitaker, "How Dutch Stormwater Management Could Mitigate Damage from Hurricanes," *60 Minutes*, July 21, 2019, https://www.cbsnews.com/news/storm-water-management-dutch-solution-henk-ovink-hurricane-damage-60-minutes-2019-07-21/.

39. Shivani Vora, "Travel Tackles Climate Change," *The New York Times*, December 2, 2018, https://www.nytimes.com/2018/12/02/climate/travel-tackles-climate-change.html?searchResultPosition=9.

40. "New Study Reveals a Greener Way to Travel: Airbnb Community Shows Environmental Benefits of Home Sharing," Airbnb, July 31, 2014, https://www.airbnb.com/press/news/

new-study-reveals-a-greener-way-to-travel-airbnb-community-shows-environmental-benefits-of-home-sharing.

41. Shivani Vora, "Travel Tackles Climate Change," *The New York Times*, December 2, 2018, https://www.nytimes.com/2018/12/02/climate/travel-tackles-climate-change.html?searchResultPosition=9.

42. Manfred Lenzen, Ya-Yen Sun, Futu Faturay, Yuan-Peng Ting, Arne Geschke, and Arunima Malik, "The Carbon Footprint of Global Tourism," *Nature Climate Change*, no. 8 522–528 (2018), https://www.nature.com/articles/s41558-018-0141-x?utm_source=commission_junction&utm_medium=affiliate.

43. Haley Britzzky, "The Most (and Least) Fuel-Efficient US Airlines," Axios, December 14, 2017, https://www.axios.com/the-most-fuel-efficient-us-airlines-1513209558-49268c44-5d73-4d38-86a3-e80a9885e0e8.html.

44. Brandon Graver and Daniel Rutherford, "Transatlantic Airline Fuel Efficiency Ranking, 2017," The International Council on Clean Transportation, white paper, September 11, 2018, https://theicct.org/publications/transatlantic-airline-fuel-efficiency-ranking-2017.

45. Lindse Oberst, "Why the Global Rise in Vegan and Plant-Based Eating Isn't a Fad (600 Percent Increase in US Vegans + Other Astounding Stats)," Food Revolution Network, January 18, 2018, https://foodrevolution.org/blog/vegan-statistics-global/.

46. Lisa Drayer, "They Might Be Better for the Planet, but Are Plant-Based Burgers Good for You?" CNN Health, August 14, 2019, https://www.cnn.com/2019/08/09/health/plant-fake-meat-burgers-good-for-you-or-not/index.html.

47. Hollee Actman Becker, "Age of First-Time Moms in US Continues to Climb," Parents, Accessed November 18, 2019, https://www.parents.com/baby/all-about-babies/age-of-first-time-moms-in-us-continues-to-climb/.

48. "Age of Mothers at Childbirth and Age-Specific Fertility," OECD, Social Policy Division, updated May 29, 2019, https://www.oecd.org/els/soc/SF_2_3_Age_mothers_childbirth.pdf.

49. Alexandra Sifferlin, "The Average Age of First-Time Moms Is Higher than Ever," *Time*, January 14, 2016, https://time.com/4181151/first-time-moms-average-age/.

50. Max Roser, "Fertility Rate," Our World in Data, December 2, 2017, https://ourworldindata.org/fertility-rate#did-china-s-one-child-policy-reduce-fertility.

51. Julia Belluz, "The Historically Low Birthrate, Explained in 3 Charts," *Vox*, May 15, 2019, https://www.vox.com/science-and-health/2018/5/22/17376536/fertility-rate-united-states-births-women.

52. "Infertility," US Department of Health & Human Services, Accessed November 18, 2019, https://www.womenshealth.gov/a-z-topics/infertility.

53. "Who Has Infertility?" Resolve, Accessed November 18, 2019, https://resolve.org/infertility-101/what-is-infertility/fast-facts/.

54. Heather Young, "Tammy Sun: Making Fertility Affordable with Carrot," So She Slays, blog, June 19, 2019, https://www.sosheslays.com/featured-collabs/2019/6/16/tammy-sun-in-making-fertility-affordable.

55. "Carrot Fertility Named to CNBC's List of 100 Barrier-Breaking Startups," MarketWatch, press release, October 9, 2018, https://www.marketwatch.com/press-release/carrot-fertility-named-to-cnbcs-list-of-100-barrier-breaking-startups-2018-10-09.

56. Aaron Orendorff, "Global Ecommerce Statistics and Trends to Launch Your Business Beyond Borders," Shopify, February 14, 2019, https://www.shopify.com/enterprise/global-ecommerce-statistics.

57. Rose Leadem, "67 Fascinating Facts about Ecommerce vs. Brick and Mortar (Infographic)," *Entrepreneur*, December 30, 2017, https://www.entrepreneur.com/article/306678.

58. Hayley Peterson, "More Than 9,100 Stores Are Closing in 2019 as the Retail Apocalypse Drags on—Here's the Full List," *Business Insider*, November 12, 2019, https://www.businessinsider.com/stores-closing-in-2019-list-2019-3#office-depot-and-officemax-50-stores-22.

59. Amy Watson, "Number of Independent Bookstores in the United States from 2009 to 2019," Statista, October 29, 2019, https://www.statista.com/statistics/282808/number-of-independent-bookstores-in-the-us/.

60. "The TJX Companies, Inc. Reports Q4 and FY19 Results; Achieves Above-Plan Comp Sales Growth of 6 Percent for Both Q4 and FY19; Exceeds Q4 EPS Expectations; Announces Plans to Increase Dividend 18% and to Buy Back $1.75 to $2.25 Billion of Stock," *Business Wire*, February 27, 2019, https://investor.tjx.com/news-releases/news-release-details/tjx-companies-inc-reports-q4-and-fy19-results-achieves-above.

61. Raquel Laneri, "Tour Nordstrom's New NYC Flagship Megastore," *New York Post*, November 6, 2019, https://nypost.com/2019/11/06/tour-nordstroms-new-nyc-flagship-megastore/; "Nordstrom Introduces Seven-Story Flagship in New York," Yahoo! News, October 25, 2019, https://news.yahoo.com/nordstrom-introduces-seven-storey-flagship-york-123606666.html.

62. "The Business of Fitness with Peloton President, William Lynch," Yahoo! Finance Video, January 9, 2019, https://finance.yahoo.com/video/business-fitness-peloton-president-william-222132236.html.

CHAPTER 6

1. "The Restaurant Workforce in the United States," Workforce Strategies Initiative, The Aspen Institute, http://www.aspenwsi.org/wordpress/wp-content/uploads/The-Restaurant-Workforce-in-the-United-States.pdf.

2. "Restaurant Industry Facts at a Glance," National Restaurant Association, Restaurant.org, https://restaurant.org/research/restaurant-statistics/restaurant-industry-facts-at-a-glance.

3. Jarrett Bellini, "The No. 1 Thing to Consider Before Opening a Restaurant," CNBC, July 6, 2016, https://www.cnbc.com/2016/01/20/heres-the-real-reason-why-most-restaurants-fail.html.

4. Adam Ozimek, "No, Most Restaurants Don't Fail in the First Year," *Forbes*, January 29, 2017, https://www.forbes.com/sites/modeledbehavior/2017/01/29/no-most-restaurants-dont-fail-in-the-first-year/#5399c7b74fcc.

5. "Restaurant Industry Facts at a Glance," National Restaurant Association, Restaurant.org, https://restaurant.org/research/restaurant-statistics/restaurant-industry-facts-at-a-glance.

6. Bethany Jean Clement, "Seattle Restaurant Classics: Why You Need to Go to Ezell's Famous Chicken," *The Seattle Times*, April 25, 2019, https://www.seattletimes.com/life/food-drink/seattle-restaurant-classics-why-you-need-to-go-to-ezells-famous-chicken/.

7. Troy Wolverton, "iPhone Sales Crater 15% in Apple's Worst Holiday Results in a Decade, and the Forecast Looks Just as Grim," *Business Insider*, January 29, 2019, https://www.businessinsider.com/apple-q1-2019-earnings-iphone-sales-revenue-eps-analysis-2019-1; Ed Hardy, "Apple's Installed Base Will Soon Pass 1.5 Billion Devices," Cult of Mac, August 1, 2019, https://www.cultofmac.com/642668/iphone-sales-apple-installed-base-ipad-mac-2019/.

8. Kif Leswing, "Apple Stock Rises on Earnings Beat," CNBC, October 30, 2019, https://www.cnbc.com/2019/10/30/apple-aapl-earnings-q4-2019.html.

9. Alex Lamachenka, "5 Types of Strategic Partnership Agreements to Help Grow Your Business," PandaDoc Blog, August 16, 2019, https://blog.pandadoc.com/strategic-partnership-agreement/.

10. Amy Watson, "Number of Subscribers to ESPN's Streaming Service (ESPN+) in the United States in 2018 and 2019," Statista, February 10, 2020, https://www.statista.com/statistics/1054451/espn-plus-subscriber-us/.

11. Hillary Russ, "Disney Sees ESPN+ Reaching Up to 12 Million Subscribers by 2024," Reuters, April 11, 2019, https://www.reuters.com/article/us-walt-disney-espn/disney-sees-espn-reaching-up-to-12-million-subscribers-by-2024-idUSKCN1RO071.

12. Adam Epstein, "As AT&T's Cord-Cutting Losses Mount, its HBO Max Streaming Service Can't Get Here Fast Enough," *Quartz*, October 28, 2019, https://qz.com/1736737/as-atts-cord-cutting-losses-mount-hbo-max-cant-get-here-fast-enough/; "Will AT&T Keep DirecTV? Pay-TV Unit Lost 1.2 Million Customers in Third Quarter," *Los Angeles Times*, October 28, 2019, https://www.latimes.com/entertainment-arts/business/story/2019-10-28/att-loses-directv-customers-activist-investor.

13. Shawn M. Carter, "HBO Max Could Hit 50 Million U.S. Subscribers in First 5 Years: AT&T." Fox Business, October 28, 2019, https://www.foxbusiness.com/media/hbo-max-could-hit-50-million-u-s-subscribers-in-first-5-years-att.

14. Matthew Ball, "Streaming Video Will Soon Look Like the Bad Old Days of TV," *The New York Times*, August 22, 2019, https://www.nytimes.com/2019/08/22/opinion/netflix-hulu-cable.html; Mark Bergen, "Jeff Bezos: Amazon Prime Video Doesn't Compete With Netflix Because Reviewers Will Just Pick Both," *Vox*, May 31, 2016, https://www.vox.com/2016/5/31/11826166/jeff-bezos-amazon-prime-video-netflix.

15. J. P. Mangalindan, "Why Amazon's Fire Phone Failed," *Fortune*, September 29, 2014, https://fortune.com/2014/09/29/why-amazons-fire-phone-failed/.

16. "See Why Target Canada Failed." YouTube video, 1:27, *USA Today*, January 15, 2015, https://www.youtube.com/watch?v=0_O5bcq1dBw&feature=youtu.be.

17. Bill Saporito, "How 2 Brothers Turned a $300 Cooler into a $450 Million Cult Brand," *Inc.*, January 27, 2016, https://www.inc.com/magazine/201602/bill-saporito/yeti-coolers-founders-roy-ryan-seiders.html.

18. "YETI: YETI Holdings Inc. Annual Income Statement," MarketWatch, Accessed November 18, 2019, https://www.marketwatch.com/investing/stock/yeti/financials.

19. Institute of Mergers, Acquisitions and Alliances, "M&A Statistics," https://imaa-institute.org/mergers-and-acquisitions-statistics/.

20. Craig Smith, "Major Disney Acquisitions Over Time | Disney Company History," updated on April 15, 2019, https://disneynews.us/important-disney-acquisitions-time-disney-history/.

21. "For Vinnie Johnson, a New Game Beckons," *Automotive News*, October 23, 2017, https://www.autonews.com/article/20171023/OEM10/171029930/for-vinnie-johnson-a-new-game-beckons.

22. "Piston Group," https://www.pistongroup.com/wp-content/uploads/2018/08/PG-Company-Profile_rev0219.pdf.

23. "Piston Group Grows with Acquisition of Irvin Automotive

Products," PRNewswire, September 28, 2016, https://www.prnewswire.com/news-releases/piston-group-grows-with-acquisition-of-irvin-automotive-products-300335619.html.

24. "Piston Group," https://www.pistongroup.com/.

CHAPTER 7

1. Drugbank "Statistics," Canadian Institutes of Health Research, https://www.drugbank.ca/stats.

2. Matej Mikulic, "World Pharmaceutical Sales 2016–2018 by Region," Statista, March 13, 2019, https://www.statista.com/statistics/272181/world-pharmaceutical-sales-by-region/.

3. Matej Mikulic, "Pfizer–Statistics & Facts," Statista, March 1, 2019, https://www.statista.com/topics/1394/pfizer/.

4. "Charles Pfizer," Pfizer: One of the World's Premier Biopharmaceutical Companies, Accessed November 18, 2019, https://web.archive.org/web/20170510151810/http://www.pfizer.com/about/history/charles_pfizer.

5. "Company History," Pfizer, Accessed November 18, 2019, https://www.pfizer.com/about/history/1951-1999.

6. Angus Liu, "From Old Behemoth Lipitor to New King Humira: Bestselling U.S. Drugs Over 25 Years," FiercePharma, May 14, 2018, https://www.fiercepharma.com/pharma/from-old-behemoth-lipitor-to-new-king-humira-u-s-best-selling-drugs-over-25-years.

7. Associated Press, "Lipitor Becomes World's Top-Selling Drug," Crain's New York Business, December 27, 2011, https://www.crainsnewyork.com/article/20111228/HEALTH_CARE/111229902/lipitor-becomes-world-s-top-selling-drug.

8. Matej Mikulic, "Pfizer's Lipitor Revenue Worldwide 2003–2018," Statista, August 9, 2019, https://www.statista.com/statistics/254341/pfizers-worldwide-viagra-revenues-since-2003/.

9. David Hunkar, "The Top 25 Global Pharmaceutical

Companies by 2011 Sales," TopForeignStocks, October 31, 2012, https://topforeignstocks.com/2012/10/31/the-top-25-pharmaceutical-companies-by-2011-sales/.

10. "Pfizer Revenue 2006-2019: PFE," Macrotrends, Accessed November 18, 2019, https://www.macrotrends.net/stocks/charts/PFE/pfizer/revenue.

11. James Currier, "Defensibility Creates the Most Value for Founders," TechCrunch, September 15, 2016, https://techcrunch.com/2016/09/15/defensibility-creates-the-most-value-for-founders/.

12. Liz Alderman, "Nespresso and Rivals Vie for Dominance in Coffee War," *The New York Times,* August 20, 2010, https://www.nytimes.com/2010/08/21/business/global/21coffee.html?.

13. "Nespresso," https://www.nestle-nespresso.com/.

14. Sarah Berger, "Self-Made Spanx Billionaire Sara Blakely Has Never Had Coffee—Here's How She Starts Her Day Instead," CNBC, June 30, 2018, https://www.cnbc.com/2018/06/29/spanx-founder-sara-blakelys-morning-routine-does-not-include-coffee.html.

15. Clare O'Connor, "How Sara Blakely of Spanx Turned $5,000 into $1 Billion," *Forbes*, March 14, 2012, https://www.forbes.com/global/2012/0326/billionaires-12-feature-united-states-spanx-sara-blakely-american-booty.html#648cfe727ea0.

16. Jane Mulkerrins, "All Spanx to Sara: Meet Sara Blakely, The Woman We Have to Thank For Trimming Our Tums and Boosting Our Bottoms," *Daily Mail*, April 8, 2013, https://www.dailymail.co.uk/home/you/article-2303499/Meet-Spanx-creator-Sarah-Blakely.html.

17. "The Story of SPANX: Company Timeline," QVC, https://www.qvc.com/footers/fa/pdf/SpanxFacts.pdf.

18. Clare O'Connor, "Watch Out, Victoria's Secret: Spanx Billionaire Sara Blakely Opens First Retail Store," *Forbes*, November 1, 2012, https://www.forbes.com/sites/clareoconnor/2012/11/01/watch-out-victorias-secret-spanx-billionaire-sara-blakely-opens-first-retail-store/#257061622b4b.

19. "Patents Assigned to Spanx, Inc.—Justia Patents Search," Justia Patents, Accessed November 18, 2019, https://patents.justia.com/assignee/spanx-inc.

20. "#23 Sara Blakely," *Forbes*, November 18, 2019, https://www.forbes.com/profile/sara-blakely/#5282803a76bb.

21. "Spanx: Retail Stores," https://www.spanx.com/retail-stores.

22. "World Class Supplier Quality—Boeing 787 Updates," Boeing Mobilizes Resources, Accessed November 18, 2019, https://787updates.newairplane.com/787-Suppliers/World-Class-Supplier-Quality.

23. Dominic Gates, "Boeing Celebrates 787 Delivery as Program's Costs Top $32 Billion," *The Seattle Times*, September 25, 2011, https://www.seattletimes.com/business/boeing-celebrates-787-delivery-as-programs-costs-top-32-billion/.

24. James Currier, "70% of Value in Tech Is Driven by Network Effects," NFX, November 28, 2017, https://medium.com/@nfx/70-of-value-in-tech-is-driven-by-network-effects-8c4788528e35.

25. James Currier, "The Network Effects Manual: 13 Different Network Effects (and Counting)," NFX, https://www.nfx.com/post/network-effects-manual.

26. Sarah Phillips, "A Brief History of Facebook," *The Guardian*, July 25, 2007, https://www.theguardian.com/technology/2007/jul/25/media.newmedia.

27. J. Clement, "Number of Monthly Active Facebook Users Worldwide as of 2nd Quarter 2019," Statista, August 9, 2019, https://www.statista.com/statistics/264810/number-of-monthly-active-facebook-users-worldwide/.

28. Alexis C. Madrigal, "Before It Conquered the World, Facebook Conquered Harvard," *The Atlantic*, February 4, 2019, https://www.theatlantic.com/technology/archive/2019/02/and-then-there-was-thefacebookcom/582004/.

29. Jordan Valinsky, Ahiza Garcia, and Tal Yellin, "Facebook's Bottomless Pit of Scandals," CNN, December 20, 2018, https://www.cnn.com/interactive/2018/12/business/facebooks-year-of-scandal/index.html; Gabriel J. X. Dance, Nicholas Confessore, and Michael LaForgia, "Facebook Gave Device Makers Deep Access to Data on Users and Friends," *The New York Times*, June 4, 2018, https://www.nytimes.com/interactive/2018/06/03/technology/

facebook-device-partners-users-friends-data.html; Sheera Frenkel, Nicholas Confessore, Cecilia Kang, Matthew Rosenberg, and Jack Nicas, "Delay, Deny and Deflect: How Facebook's Leaders Fought Through Crisis," *The New York Times*, November 14, 2018, https://www.nytimes.com/2018/11/14/technology/facebook-data-russia-election-racism.html.

30. Cecilia Kang, "F.T.C. Approves Facebook Fine of About $5 Billion," *The New York Times*, July 12, 2019, https://www.nytimes.com/2019/07/12/technology/facebook-ftc-fine.html.

31. Queenie Wong, "Facebook Is Still Growing Despite Criticism About Political Ads," CNET, October 30, 2019, https://www.cnet.com/news/facebook-is-still-growing-despite-criticism-about-political-ads/.

32. Andrew Hutchinson, "New Report Shows Facebook Usage Dropped for a Second Straight Year in the US," *Social Media Today*, March 8, 2019, https://www.socialmediatoday.com/news/new-report-shows-facebook-usage-dropped-for-a-second-straight-year-in-the-u/550019/.

33. Murali Krishnan, "What Is an 'Internet Marketplace'? What Is the Definition?," Quora, March 15, 2011, https://www.quora.com/What-is-an-internet-marketplace-What-is-the-definition.

34. "About Thomas," ThomasNet, Accessed November 18, 2019, https://business.thomasnet.com/about.

35. James Currier, "From Social Networks to Market Networks," TechCrunch, June 27, 2015, https://techcrunch.com/2015/06/27/from-social-to-market-networks/; James Currier, "The Next 10 Years Will Be About 'Market Networks,'" NFX, https://www.nfx.com/post/10-years-about-market-networks.

36. "#49 Adi Tatarko," *Forbes*, June 3, 2019, https://www.forbes.com/profile/adi-tatarko/#1a0c1d631454.

37. Sarah Leary, "Celebrating Lorelei, America's First Nextdoor Neighborhood." Nextdoor blog, May 22, 2017, https://blog.nextdoor.com/2017/05/22/celebrating-lorelei-americas-first-nextdoor-neighborhood/; Ben Popper, "The Anti-Facebook: One in Four American Neighborhoods Are Now Using This Private Social Network," *The Verge*, August 18, 2014, https://

www.theverge.com/2014/8/18/6030393/nextdoor-private-social-network-40000-neighborhoods; Ben Popper, "Nextdoor—a Private, Localized Social Network—Is Now Used in Over 100,000 US Neighborhoods," *The Verge*, June 23, 2016, https://www.theverge.com/2016/6/23/12005456/nextdoor-100000-neighborhood-social-network-app-changes-business-plan-expansion; Paul Sawers, "Neighborhood Social Network Nextdoor Raises $123 Million at $2.1 Billion Valuation," Venture Beat, May 14, 2019, https://venturebeat.com/2019/05/14/neighborhood-social-network-nextdoor-raises-123-million-at-2-1-billion-valuation/.

CHAPTER 8

1. "Execution Without Strategy Is Aimless," Albu Consulting Strategy Management, https://albu-strategymanagement.com/2018/11/execution-without-strategy-is-aimless/.

2. JasperRibbers, "The Airbnb Founder Story: From Selling Cereals to a $25B Company," Get Paid for Your Pad, August 8, 2019, https://getpaidforyourpad.com/blog/the-airbnb-founder-story.

3. Dara Khosrowshahi, "Uber's New Cultural Norms," Uber Newsroom, November 8, 2017, https://www.uber.com/newsroom/ubers-new-cultural-norms/.

4. Stephen McBride, "Netflix's Worst Nightmare Has Come True," *Forbes*, July 8, 2019, https://www.forbes.com/sites/stephenmcbride1/2019/07/08/netflixs-worst-nightmare-has-come-true/#a5c337c396d2.

5. David Witt, "Only 14% of Employees Understand Their Company's Strategy and Direction," Blanchard LeaderChat, May 21, 2012, https://leaderchat.org/2012/05/21/only-14-of-employees-understand-their-companys-strategy-and-direction/.

6. Ken Lin, "The Importance of Transparency to Company Morale." *Inc.*, March 24, 2015, https://www.inc.com/ken-lin/the-importance-of-transparency-to-company-morale.html.

7. Laura Montini, "Jack Dorsey: Be Totally Transparent with

Employees." *Inc.*, November 5, 2013, https://www.inc.com/laura-montini/why-600-employees-know-everything-about-square-at-all-times.html.

8. Satya Nadella, *Hit Refresh: The Quest to Rediscover Microsoft's Soul and Imagine a Better Future for Everyone* (New York City: HarperBusiness, 2017): 100.

9. Nicholas Carlson, "The Real History of Twitter," *Business Insider*, April 13, 2011, https://www.businessinsider.com/how-twitter-was-founded-2011-4.

10. Ben Woods, "Instagram—a Brief History," The Next Web, June 21, 2013, https://thenextweb.com/magazine/2013/06/21/instagram-a-brief-history/.

11. Knowlton Thomas, "A Brief History of Slack." Techvibes, September 26, 2015, https://techvibes.com/2015/09/25/a-brief-history-of-slack-2015-09-25.

12. Aimee Groth, "19 Amazing Ways CEO Howard Schultz Saved Starbucks," *Business Insider*, June 19, 2011, https://www.businessinsider.com/howard-schultz-turned-starbucks-around-2011-6?op=1.

13. Johnny Davis, "How Lego Clicked: The Super Brand That Reinvented Itself," *The Guardian*, June 4, 2017, https://www.theguardian.com/lifeandstyle/2017/jun/04/how-lego-clicked-the-super-brand-that-reinvented-itself.

14. Martin Lindstrom, "Here's How an Old Pair of Sneakers Saved Lego," *Fortune*, March 13, 2016, https://fortune.com/2016/03/13/heres-how-an-old-pair-of-sneakers-saved-lego.

15. Lindstrom, 2016.

16. "The Lego Movie," Box Office Mojo, Accessed November 18, 2019, https://www.boxofficemojo.com/movies/?id=lego.htm.

17. "Lego Overtakes Ferrari as the World's Most Powerful Brand," Brand Finance, http://brandfinance.com/press-releases/lego-overtakes-ferrari-as-the-worlds-most-powerful-brand/.

18. "Annual Report 2018," The LEGO Group, https://www.lego.com/cdn/cs/aboutus/assets/blt02144956ae00afa1/Annual_Report_2018_ENG.pdf.

19. Joel Deering, "Top 10 Head Coach–QB Duos of All Time," Fourth Quarter Sports, February 2, 2019, https://fourthquartersports. org/2019/02/02/top-10-head-coach-qb-duos-of-all-time/.

20. Randy Roberts, *The Rock, the Curse, and the Hub: A Random History of Boston Sports* (Cambridge: Harvard University Press, 2005).

21. Dan Moskowitz, "10 Most Valuable NFL Teams 2019: Cowboys Lead the Pack," Investopedia, October 6, 2019, https://www. investopedia.com/articles/personal-finance/022315/5-mostvaluable-nfl-franchises.asp.

About the Author

BRAD CHASE has had a broad and extensive business career. He has advised leaders of businesses of many different sizes, from startups to Fortune 500 firms, and in many different kinds of markets, from mobile and education to enterprises and consumer services. Some of the companies he has worked with include GE, Telstra, VMWare, Mozy (a subsidiary of EMC), Blucora, Sonos, Vizrea, and Crisply. He has also held leadership positions on the boards of many companies and nonprofit organizations, including Expedia, Ooyala, DreamBox, Brooks, Boys & Girls Clubs of King County, and The Nature Conservancy. As a public speaker, Brad has spoken about his particular theory on business strategy, Strategy First, to executives at large and small businesses, to incubators, at conferences, and to students at topflight MBA programs.

Before consulting, board work, and speaking, Brad spent 14 years at Microsoft, finishing his tenure as a senior vice president and executive officer managing a team of over 4,000. From April 1999 until mid-2002, Brad led MSN.com's transformation from an internet service to the worldwide traffic and search leader. Under his leadership at MSN, search traffic, revenue, and internal team morale all more than doubled.

Prior to MSN, Brad led marketing for the client and server business for Windows 2000, Windows 98, and Internet Explorer (IE) versions one through five. Brad's marketing team introduced a new, more profitable product strategy for the server and client businesses, successfully launched Windows 98 and Windows 2000, and helped IE become the market leader. Brad also developed and led the marketing strategy, execution, and worldwide, record-breaking launch for Windows 95, which is often considered the event and product that ushered computers and software into the mainstream. Brad and his team won numerous awards for the Windows 95 marketing effort. Brad also oversaw the launches for both MS-DOS 5 and MS-DOS 6 and was the first marketing leader for Microsoft Office.

In addition to his nonprofit board work and personal giving, Brad has donated tens of thousands of dollars to charitable causes through his side company Entspire, maker of the fun and fascinating origins game Orijinz.

Prior to joining Microsoft in 1987, Brad worked as a sales representative for Boise Cascade's office products division. He holds an MBA from Northwestern's Kellogg School of Management and a BS degree from the University of California at Berkeley.

More about Brad can be found on his website: bradchase.net.